Luce County, Michigan

Johnathan Black

Contents

Articles

Overview of the County — 1
- Luce County, Michigan — 1
- Michigan — 5

History — 37
- History of Michigan — 37
- Cyrus G. Luce — 45

Geography — 47
- Upper Peninsula of Michigan — 47
- Lake Superior — 68

Cities/ Towns in Luce County — 80
- Newberry, Michigan — 80
- Columbus Township, Luce County, Michigan — 84
- Lakefield Township, Luce County, Michigan — 87
- McMillan Township, Luce County, Michigan — 89
- Pentland Township, Michigan — 92

Nearby Counties — 94
- Alger County, Michigan — 94
- Chippewa County, Michigan — 100
- Mackinac County, Michigan — 105
- Schoolcraft County, Michigan — 113

Attractions — 118

Tahquamenon Falls	118
Tahquamenon Falls State Park	121
Tahquamenon River	123
Muskallonge Lake State Park	125

Transportation   **126**

Sault Ste. Marie Airport	126

References

Article Sources and Contributors	129
Image Sources, Licenses and Contributors	130

Overview of the County

Luce County, Michigan

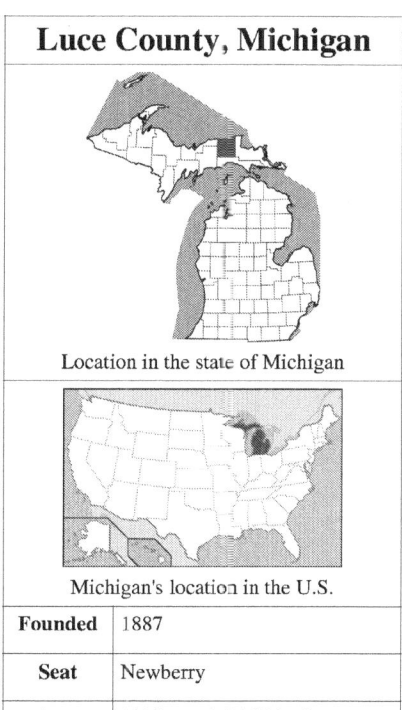

Luce County, Michigan	
Location in the state of Michigan	
Michigan's location in the U.S.	
Founded	1887
Seat	Newberry
Area - Total - Land - Water	1912 sq mi (4952 km²) 903 sq mi (2339 km²) 1009 sq mi (2613 km²), 52.76%
Population - **(2000)** - **Density**	7024 8/sq mi (3/km²)

Luce County is a county in the U.S. state of Michigan. As of the 2000 census, the population was 7,024. The county seat is Newberry. In 2002, Newberry was designated as the moose capital of Michigan by the state legislature. The county is named after former Michigan Governor Cyrus G. Luce (R).

Luce County Government Building

Demographics

As of the census of 2000, there were 7,024 people, 2,481 households, and 1,739 families residing in the county. The population density was 8 people per square mile (3/km²). There were 4,008 housing units at an average density of 4 per square mile (2/km²). The racial makeup of the county was 82.84% White, 7.52% Black or African American, 5.54% Native American, 0.36% Asian, 0.03% Pacific Islander, 0.47% from other races, and 3.25% from two or more races. 1.75% of the population were Hispanic or Latino of any race. 20.2% were of German, 10.2% English, 10.1% American, 7.8% Irish and 7.7% French ancestry. 97.0% spoke English and 2.3% Spanish as their first language.

There were 2,481 households out of which 29.50% had children under the age of 18 living with them, 57.90% were married couples living together, 8.50% had a female householder with no husband present, and 29.90% were non-families. 26.30% of all households were made up of individuals and 12.10% had someone living alone who was 65 years of age or older. The average household size was 2.40 and the average family size was 2.86.

In the county the population was spread out with 21.40% under the age of 18, 8.60% from 18 to 24, 30.50% from 25 to 44, 24.10% from 45 to 64, and 15.40% who were 65 years of age or older. The median age was 39 years. For every 100 females there were 124.70 males. For every 100 females age 18 and over, there were 132.80 males.

The median income for a household in the county was $32,031, and the median income for a family was $36,359. Males had a median income of $31,427 versus $21,101 for females. The per capita income for the county was $16,828. About 12.00% of families and 14.90% of the population were below the poverty line, including 20.10% of those under age 18 and 8.40% of those age 65 or over.

Geography

- According to the U.S. Census Bureau, the county has a total area of 1,912 square miles (4,952 km²), of which, 903 square miles (2,339 km²) of it is land and 1,009 square miles (2,613 km²) of it (52.76%) is water.
- Luce County is part of the Upper Peninsula of Michigan.

Highways

Michigan Highways

- M-28
- M-117
- M-123

Intercounty Highways

- H-33
- H-37
- H-44
- H-58

Adjacent counties

- Chippewa County (east)
- Mackinac County (south)
- Schoolcraft County (southwest)
- Alger County (west)
- Thunder Bay District, Ontario (north, water boundary only, in Lake Superior)

Government

The county government operates the jail, maintains rural roads, operates the major local courts, keeps files of deeds and mortgages, maintains vital records, administers public health regulations, and participates with the state in the provision of welfare and other social services. The county board of commissioners controls the budget but has only limited authority to make laws or ordinances. In Michigan, most local government functions — police and fire, building and zoning, tax assessment, street maintenance, etc. — are the responsibility of individual cities and townships.

Luce County elected officials

- Prosecuting Attorney: Peter Tazelaar II
- Sheriff: Kevin R. Erickson
- County Clerk/Register of Deeds: Kathy S. Mahar
- County Treasurer: Deborah Johnson

(information as of September 2005)

Cities, villages, and townships

Villages

- Newberry

Townships

- Columbus
- Lakefield
- McMillan
- Pentland

Bibliography

- Clarke Historical Library, Central Michigan University, Bibliography on Luce County. [1]

Geographical coordinates: 46°17′N 85°20′W

Michigan

State of Michigan

Flag

Seal

Nickname(s): The Great Lakes State, The Wolverine State

Motto(s): Si quaeris peninsulam amoenam circumspice (If you seek a pleasant peninsula, look about you)

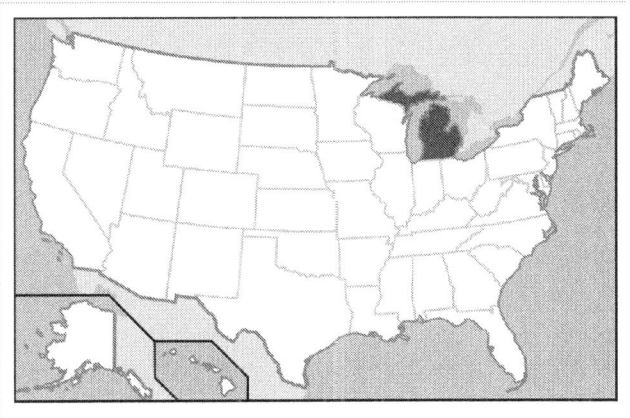

Official language(s)	None (English, *de-facto*)
Demonym	Michigander Michiganian
Capital	Lansing
Largest city	Detroit
Largest metro area	Metro Detroit
Area	Ranked 11th in the US
- Total	97,990 sq mi (253,793 km^2)
- Width	386 miles (621 km)

- Length	456 miles (734 km)
- % water	41.5
- Latitude	41° 41' N to 48° 18' N
- Longitude	82° 7' W to 90° 25' W
Population	Ranked 8th in the US
- Total	10,045,697 (2008 est.)
- Density	179/sq mi (67.55/km^2) Ranked 16th in the US
- Median income	$44,627 (21st)
Elevation	
- Highest point	Mount Arvon 1,979 ft (603 m)
- Mean	902 ft (275 m)
- Lowest point	Lake Erie 571 ft (174 m)
Admission to Union	January 26, 1837 (26th)
Governor	Jennifer Granholm (D)
Lieutenant Governor	John D. Cherry (D)
Legislature	Michigan Legislature
- Upper house	Senate
- Lower house	House of Representatives
U.S. Senators	• Carl Levin (D) • Debbie Stabenow (D)
U.S. House delegation	8 Democrats 7 Republicans (list)
Time zones	
- most of state	Eastern: UTC-5/-4
- 4 U.P. counties	Central: UTC-6/-5
Abbreviations	MI Mich. US-MI
Website	http://www.michigan.gov

Michigan (ˈ /'mɪʃɪɡən/) is a U.S. state located in the Great Lakes Region of the United States of America. The name Michigan is a French corruption of the Ojibwe word *mishigama*, meaning "large water" or "large lake".

Michigan is the eighth most populous state in the United States. It has the longest freshwater shoreline of any political subdivision in the world, being bounded by four of the five Great Lakes, plus Lake Saint Clair. In 2005, Michigan ranked third among US states for the number of registered recreational boats, behind California and Florida. Michigan has 64,980 inland lakes and ponds. A person in the state is never more than six miles (10 km) from a natural water source or more than 87.2 miles (140.3 km) from a Great Lakes shoreline. It is the largest state by total area east of the Mississippi River.

Michigan is the only state to consist entirely of two peninsulas. The Lower Peninsula, to which the name Michigan was originally applied, is often dubbed "the mitten" by residents, owing to its shape. The Upper Peninsula (often referred to as "The U.P.") is separated from the Lower Peninsula by the Straits of Mackinac, a five-mile (8 km)-wide channel that joins Lake Huron to Lake Michigan. The Upper Peninsula is economically important for tourism and natural resources.

History

See also: Timeline of Michigan history, History of railroads in Michigan, History of Michigan, and History of Detroit

Michigan was home to Native American cultures before colonization by Europeans. When the first European explorers arrived, the most populous and influential tribes were Algonquian peoples, specifically, the *Ottawa*, the *Anishnabe* (called *Chippewa* in French, after their language *Ojibwe*), and the *Potawatomi*. The Anishnabe, whose numbers are estimated to have been between 25,000 and 35,000, were the most populous.

Although the Anishnabe were well-established in Michigan's Upper Peninsula and northern Lower Peninsula, they also inhabited northern Ontario, northern Wisconsin, southern Manitoba, and northern and north-central Minnesota. The Ottawa lived primarily south of the Straits of Mackinac in northern and western Michigan, while the Potawatomi were primarily in the southwest. The three nations co-existed peacefully as part of a loose confederation called the Council of Three Fires. Other First Nations people in Michigan, in the south and east, were the *Mascouten*, the *Menominee*, the *Miami*, and the Wyandot, who are better known by their French name, *Huron*.

17th century

French *voyageurs*, explored and settled in Michigan in the 17th century. The first Europeans to reach what later became Michigan were those of Étienne Brûlé's expedition in 1622. The first permanent European settlement was founded in 1668 on the site where Father (*Père*, in French) Jacques Marquette established Sault Ste. Marie, Michigan as a Catholic mission to minister to the Ottawa Indians, and to serve as a regional headquarters for further Catholic missionary activities in the upper Great Lakes area. It was here that the first European building was erected in Michigan, within the US Midwest, and also within what is now the Canadian province of Ontario.

Soon afterward, in 1671 the outlying mission of Saint Ignace was founded approximately 50 miles (80 km) south. Then in 1675, French Catholic missionaries founded Marquette approximately 200 miles (320 km) to the west of Sault Ste. Marie, on the south shore of Lake Superior. Together with Sault Ste. Marie, these three original Jesuit missions are the first three European-founded cities in Michigan. Jesuit missionaries were well received by the Indian populations in the area, with relatively few difficulties or hostilities. "The Soo" (Sault Ste. Marie) has the distinction of being the oldest city in both Michigan and Ontario. It was split into two cities in 1818, a year after the U.S.-Canada boundary in the Great Lakes was finally established by the U.S.-U.K. Joint Border Commission following the War of 1812.

In 1679, Lord La Salle of France directed the construction of the *Griffin*, the first European sailing vessel built on the upper Great Lakes. That same year, La Salle built Fort Miami at present-day St. Joseph.

18th century

In 1701, French explorer and army officer Antoine de la Mothe Cadillac founded Le Fort Ponchartrain du Détroit or "Fort Ponchartrain on-the-Strait" on the strait, known as the Detroit River, between lakes Saint Clair and Erie. Cadillac had convinced King Louis XIV's chief minister, Louis Phélypeaux, Comte de Pontchartrain, that a permanent community there would strengthen French control over the upper Great Lakes and repel British aspirations. Cadillac served as the French governor of Louisiana from 1710 to 1716.

Michigan in 1718, Guillaume de L'Isle map, approximate state area highlighted.

The hundred soldiers and workers who accompanied Cadillac built a fort enclosing one arpent (about 0.85 acres (3400 m^2), the equivalent of just under 200 feet (61 m) per side) and named it Fort Pontchartrain. Cadillac's wife, Marie Thérèse Guyon, soon moved to Detroit, becoming one of the first European women to settle in the Michigan wilderness. The town quickly became a major fur-trading and shipping post. The *Église de Saint-Anne* (Church of Saint Ann) was founded the same year. While the original building does not survive, the congregation of that name continues to be active today.

At the same time, the French strengthened Fort Michilimackinac at the Straits of Mackinac to better control their lucrative fur-trading empire. By the mid-18th century, the French also occupied forts at present-day Niles and Sault Ste. Marie, though most of the rest of the region remained unsettled by

Europeans.

From 1660 to the end of French rule, Michigan was part of the Royal Province of New France. In 1759, following the Battle of the Plains of Abraham in the French and Indian War (1754–1763), Québec City fell to British forces. This marked Britain's victory in the Seven Years War. Under the 1763 Treaty of Paris, Michigan and the rest of New France east of the Mississippi River passed to Great Britain.

During the American Revolutionary War, Detroit was an important British supply center. Most of the inhabitants were French-Canadians or Native Americans, many of whom had been allied with the French. Because of imprecise cartography and unclear language defining the boundaries in the 1763 Treaty of Paris, the British retained control of Detroit and Michigan after the American Revolution. When Quebec split into Lower and Upper Canada in 1790, Michigan was part of Kent County, Upper Canada. It held its first democratic elections in August 1792 to send delegates to the new provincial parliament at Newark (now Niagara-on-the-Lake).

Under terms negotiated in the 1794 Jay Treaty, Britain withdrew from Detroit and Michilimackinac in 1796. Questions remained over the boundary for many years, and the United States did not have uncontested control of the Upper Peninsula and Drummond Island until 1818 and 1847, respectively.

19th century

During the War of 1812, Michigan Territory (effectively consisting of Detroit and the surrounding area) was captured by the British and nominally returned to Upper Canada. United States forces pushed the British out in 1813 and moved into Canada.

The Treaty of Ghent implemented the policy of *Status Quo Ante Bellum* or "Just as Things Were Before the War." That meant Michigan would remain as part of the United States, and the agreement to establish a joint US-UK boundary commission also remained valid. Subsequent to the findings of that commission in 1817, control of the Upper Peninsula and of islands in the St. Clair River delta was transferred from Ontario to Michigan in 1818. Mackinac Island (to which the British had moved their Michilimackinac army base) was transferred to the U.S. in 1847.

The population grew slowly until the opening of the Erie Canal in New York State 1825 brought a large influx of settlers. Commodities such as grain, lumber, and iron ore could be shipped via the Great Lakes through the Erie Canal and Hudson River. By the 1830s, Michigan had 80,000 residents. More than enough to apply and qualify for statehood. The waterway connection among the Great Lakes states increased the wealth of all.

In October 1835 the people approved the Constitution of 1835, thereby forming a state government, although Congressional recognition was delayed pending resolution of a boundary dispute with Ohio. Both states claimed a 468-square-mile (1,210 km^2) strip of land that included the newly incorporated city of Toledo on Lake Erie and an

Lumbering pines in the late 1800s

area to the west then known as the "Great Black Swamp". The dispute came to be called the Toledo War. Michigan and Ohio militia maneuvered in the area but never exchanged fire. Congress awarded the "Toledo Strip" to Ohio. Michigan received the western part of the Upper Peninsula as a concession and formally entered the Union on January 26, 1837.

The Upper Peninsula proved to be a rich source of lumber, iron, and copper. These were among the state's most sought-after natural resources. Geologist Douglass Houghton and land surveyor William Austin Burt were among the first to document many of these resources. Developers rushed to the state. Michigan led the nation in lumber production from 1850s to the 1880s.

The first official meeting of the Republican Party took place July 6, 1854 in Jackson, Michigan, where the party adopted its platform. Michigan made a significant contribution to the Union in the American Civil War and sent more than forty regiments of volunteers to the Federal armies.

Communities and the state rapidly set up systems for public education, including founding the University of Michigan, for a classical academic education, and Ypsilanti Normal College (now Eastern Michigan University, for the training of teachers. Michigan State University in East Lansing was founded as a land-grant college. In the early 20th century, Michigan was the first state to offer a four-year curriculum in a normal college.

20th century to present

See also: History of Ford Motor Company

Michigan's economy underwent a transformation at the turn of the 20th century. The birth of the automotive industry, with Henry Ford's first plant in Highland Park, marked the beginning of a new era in transportation. Like the steamship and railroad, it was a far-reaching development. More than the forms of public transportation, the automobile transformed private life. It became the major industry of Detroit and Michigan, and permanently altered the socio-economic life of the United States and much of the world.

With the growth, the auto industry created jobs in Detroit that attracted immigrants from Europe and migrants from across the country, including both whites and blacks from the rural South. By 1910 Detroit was the fourth largest city in the nation. Residential housing was in short supply, and it took years for the market to catch up with the population boom. By the 1930s, so many immigrants had arrived that more than 30 languages were spoken in the public schools, and ethnic communities celebrated in annual heritage festivals.

Many African Americans moved to Detroit as one of the destinations in the Great Migration from the South, as they could find better work there. Over the years they contributed greatly to its diverse urban culture. African Americans from Detroit created national popular music trends, such as the influential Motown Sound of the 1960s led by a variety of individual singers and groups.

Grand Rapids, the second-largest city in Michigan, is also an important center of manufacturing. Since 1838, the city had also been noted for its thriving furniture industry. Started because of ready sources of lumber, the furniture industry declined in the late 20th century through competition with other regional firms and overseas industry.

Michigan held its first United States presidential primary election in 1910. With its rapid growth in industry, it was an important center of union industry-wide organizing, such as the rise of the United Auto Workers.

In 1920 WWJ in Detroit became the first radio station in the United States to regularly broadcast commercial programs. Throughout that decade, some of the country's largest and most ornate skyscrapers were built in the city. Particularly noteworthy are the Fisher Building, Cadillac Place, and the Guardian Building, each of which is a National Historic Landmarks (NHL).

Detroit boomed through the 1950s, at one point doubling its population in a decade. After World War II, housing development grew outside cities. Newly built highways allowed commuters to navigate the region more easily. In Detroit as elsewhere, many began to move to newer housing in the suburbs.

Michigan is the leading auto-producing state in the U.S., although some of the industry has shifted to less-expensive labor in the Southern United States and overseas. With more than ten million residents, Michigan remains a large and influential state, ranking eighth in population among the fifty states.

The Metro Detroit area in the southeast corner of the state is the largest metropolitan area in Michigan (roughly 50% of the population resides there) and one of the ten largest metropolitan areas in the country. The Grand Rapids/Holland/Muskegon metropolitan area on the west side of the state is the fastest-growing metro area in the state, with over 1.3 million residents as of 2006.

Metro Detroit's population is growing. Detroit's population is stabilizing with a strong redevelopment in the city's central district with a significant rise in population in its outskirts are contributing to some population inflow. A period of economic transition, especially in manufacturing, has caused economic difficulties in the region since the recession of 2001.

Government

See also: List of Governors of Michigan and United States congressional delegations from Michigan

State government

Main article: Government of Michigan

Michigan is governed as a republic, with three branches of government: the executive branch consisting of the Governor of Michigan and the other independently elected constitutional officers; the legislative branch consisting of the House of Representatives and Senate; and the judicial branch consisting of the one court of justice. The state also allows direct participation of the electorate by initiative, referendum, recall, and ratification. Lansing is the state capital and is home to all three branches of state government.

The Governor of Michigan and the other state constitutional officers serve four-year terms and may be re-elected only once. The current Governor is Jennifer Granholm. Michigan has two official Governor's Residences; one is in Lansing, and the other is at Mackinac Island.

The Michigan Legislature consists of a 38-member Senate and 110-member House of Representatives. Senators serve four-year terms and Representatives two. The Michigan State Capitol was dedicated in 1879 and has hosted the state's executive and legislative branches ever since.

Law

The Michigan Court System consists of two courts with primary jurisdiction (the Circuit Courts and the District Courts), one intermediate level appellate court (the Michigan Court of Appeals), and the Michigan Supreme Court. There are several administrative courts and specialized courts. The Michigan Constitution provides for voter initiative and referendum (Article II, § 9, defined as "the power to propose laws and to enact and reject laws, called the initiative, and the power to approve or reject laws enacted by the legislature, called the referendum. The power of initiative extends only to laws which the legislature may enact under this constitution").

In 1846 Michigan was the first state in the Union, as well as the first English-speaking government in the world, to abolish the death penalty. Historian David Chardavoyne has suggested that the movement to abolish capital punishment in Michigan grew as a result of enmity toward the state's neighbor, Canada. Under British rule, it made public executions a regular practice.

Politics

See also: Elections in Michigan and Political party strength in Michigan

Michigan Governor Jennifer Granholm (D)

Presidential elections results

Year	Republicans	Democrats
2008	40.89% 2,048,639	**57.33%** 2,872,579
2004	47.81% 2,313,746	**51.23%** 2,479,183
2000	46.14% 1,953,139	**51.28%** 2,170,418
1996	38.48% 1,481,212	**51.69%** 1,989,653
1992	36.38% 1,554,940	**43.77%** 1,871,182
1988	**53.57%** 1,965,486	45.67% 1,675,783
1984	**59.23%** 2,251,571	40.24% 1,529,638
1980	**48.99%** 1,915,225	42.50% 1,661,532
1976	**51.83%** 1,893,742	46.44% 1,696,714
1972	**56.20%** 1,961,721	41.81% 1,459,435
1968	41.46% 1,370,665	**48.18%** 1,593,082
1964	33.10% 1,060,152	**66.70%** 2,136,615
1960	48.84% 1,620,428	**50.85%** 1,687,269

Voters in the state elect candidates from both major parties. Economic issues are important in Michigan elections. The three-term Republican Governor John Engler (1991–2003) preceded the current

Democratic Governor Jennifer Granholm. The state has re-elected its current Republican Attorney General Mike Cox since 2003. Michigan supported the election of Republican Presidents Ronald Reagan and George H.W. Bush.

However, the state has supported Democrats in the last five presidential election cycles. In 2008, Barack Obama carried the state over John McCain, winning Michigan's seventeen electoral votes with 57% of the vote. Democrats have won each of the last three, nine of the last ten, and fifteen of the last eighteen U.S. Senate elections in Michigan with confidence on national economic issues posing a challenge. Republican strength is greatest in the western, northern, and rural parts of the state, especially in the Grand Rapids area. Republicans also do well in suburban Detroit, which tends to be an important factor in deciding statewide elections. Democrats are strongest in the east, especially in the cities of Detroit, Ann Arbor, Flint, and Saginaw.

Historically, the first formal meeting of the Republican Party took place in Jackson, Michigan on July 6, 1854 and the party thereafter dominated Michigan until the Great Depression. In the 1912 election, Michigan was one of the six states to support progressive Republican and third-party candidate Theodore Roosevelt for President after he lost the Republican nomination to William Howard Taft.

Michigan remained fairly reliably Republican at the presidential level for much of the 20th century. It was part of Greater New England, the northern tier of states settled chiefly by migrants from New England who carried their culture with them. The state was one of only a handful to back Wendell Willkie over Franklin Roosevelt in 1940, and supported Thomas E. Dewey in his losing bid against Harry Truman in 1948. Michigan went to the Democrats in presidential elections during the 1960s, and voted for Republican Richard Nixon in 1972.

Michigan was the home of Gerald Ford, the 38th President of the United States. He was born in Nebraska and moved as an infant to Grand Rapids, Michigan, and grew up there. The Gerald R. Ford Museum is located in Grand Rapids.

Administrative divisions

Main article: Administrative divisions of Michigan

See also: List of Michigan county seats, List of counties in Michigan, and List of municipalities in Michigan (by population)

State government is decentralized among three tiers — statewide, county and township. Counties are administrative divisions of the state, and townships are administrative divisions of a county. Both of them exercise state government authority, localized to meet the particular needs of their jurisdictions, as provided by state law. There are 83 counties in Michigan.

Cities, state universities, and villages are vested with home rule powers of varying degrees. Home rule cities can generally do anything that is not prohibited by law. The fifteen state universities have broad power and can do anything within the parameters of their status as educational institutions that is not prohibited by the state constitution. Villages, by contrast, have limited home rule and are not completely autonomous from the county and township in which they are located.

There are two types of township in Michigan: *general law* township and *charter*. Charter township status was created by the Legislature in 1947 and grants additional powers and stream-lined administration in order to provide greater protection against annexation by a city. As of April 2001, there were 127 charter townships in Michigan. In general, charter townships have many of the same powers as a city but without the same level of obligations. For example, a charter township can have its own fire department, water and sewer department, police department, and so on—just like a city—but it is not *required* to have those things, whereas cities *must* provide those services. Charter townships can opt to use county-wide services instead, such as deputies from the county sheriff's office instead of a home-based force of ordinance officers.

Geography

Further information: Geography of Michigan, Protected areas of Michigan, and List of Michigan state parks

Michigan consists of two peninsulas that lie between 82°30' to about 90°30' west longitude, and are separated by the Straits of Mackinac. The 45th parallel north runs through the state—marked by highway signs and the Polar-Equator Trail—along a line including Mission Point Light near Traverse City, the towns of Gaylord and Alpena and Menominee in the Upper Peninsula. With the exception of two small areas that are drained by the Mississippi River by way of the Wisconsin River in the Upper Peninsula and by way of the Kankakee-Illinois River in the Lower Peninsula, Michigan is drained by the Great Lakes-St. Lawrence watershed and is the only state with the majority of its land thus drained.

The Great Lakes that border Michigan from east to west are Lake Erie, Lake Huron, Lake Michigan and Lake Superior. It has more lighthouses than any other state. The state is bounded on the south by the states of Ohio and Indiana, sharing land and water boundaries with both. Michigan's western boundaries are almost entirely water boundaries, from south to north, with Illinois and Wisconsin in Lake Michigan; then a land boundary with Wisconsin and the Upper Peninsula, that is principally demarcated by the Menominee and Montreal Rivers; then water boundaries again, in Lake Superior, with Wisconsin and Minnesota to the west, capped around by the Canadian province of Ontario to the north and east.

Aerial view of Sleeping Bear Dunes.

Tahquamenon Falls in the Upper Peninsula of Michigan

The heavily forested Upper Peninsula is relatively mountainous in the west. The Porcupine Mountains, which are part of one of the oldest mountain chains in the world, rise to an altitude of almost 2,000 feet (610 m) above sea level and form the watershed between the streams flowing into Lake Superior and Lake Michigan. The surface on either side of this range is rugged. The state's highest point, in the Huron Mountains northwest of Marquette, is Mount Arvon at 1979 feet (603 m). The peninsula is as large as Connecticut, Delaware, Massachusetts, and Rhode Island combined but has fewer than 330,000 inhabitants. They are sometimes called "Yoopers" (from "U.P.'ers"), and their speech (the "Yooper dialect") has been heavily influenced by the numerous Scandinavian and Canadian immigrants who settled the area during the lumbering and mining boom of the late 19th century.

The Lower Peninsula, shaped like a mitten, is 277 miles (446 km) long from north to south and 195 miles (314 km) from east to west and occupies nearly two-thirds of the state's land area. The surface of the peninsula is generally level, broken by conical hills and glacial moraines usually not more than a few hundred feet tall. It is divided by a low water divide running north and south. The larger portion of the state is on the west of this and gradually slopes toward Lake Michigan. The highest point in the Lower Peninsula is either Briar Hill at 1705 feet (520 m), or one of several points nearby in the vicinity of Cadillac. The lowest point is the surface of Lake Erie at 571 feet (174 m).

The Pointe Mouillee State Game Area

The geographic orientation of Michigan's peninsulas makes for a long distance between the ends of the state. Ironwood, in the far western Upper Peninsula, lies 630 highway miles (1,015 km) from Lambertville in the Lower Peninsula's southeastern corner. The geographic isolation of the Upper Peninsula from Michigan's political and population centers makes the U.P. culturally and economically distinct. Occasionally U.P. residents have called for secession from Michigan and establishment as a new state to be called "Superior".

A feature of Michigan that gives it the distinct shape of a mitten is the Thumb. This peninsula projects out into Lake Huron and the Saginaw Bay. The geography of the Thumb is mainly flat with a few rolling hills. Other peninsulas of Michigan include the Keweenaw Peninsula, making up the Copper Country region of the state. The Leelanau Peninsula lies in the Northern Lower Michigan region. *See Also Michigan Regions*

Little Sable Point Light south of Pentwater, Michigan.

Numerous lakes and marshes mark both peninsulas, and the coast is much indented. Keweenaw Bay, Whitefish Bay, and the Big and Little Bays De Noc are the principal indentations on the Upper Peninsula. The Grand and Little Traverse, Thunder, and Saginaw bays indent the Lower Peninsula. Michigan has the ninth longest shoreline of any state—3224 miles (5189 km), including 1056 miles (1699 km) of island shoreline.

The state has numerous large islands, the principal ones being the North Manitou and South Manitou, Beaver, and Fox groups in Lake Michigan; Isle Royale and Grande Isle in Lake Superior; Marquette, Bois Blanc, and Mackinac islands in Lake Huron; and Neebish, Sugar, and Drummond islands in St. Mary's River. Michigan has about 150 lighthouses, the most of any U.S. state. The first lighthouses in Michigan were built between 1818 and 1822. They were built to project light at night and to serve as a landmark during the day to safely guide the passenger ships and freighters traveling the Great Lakes. See Lighthouses in the United States.

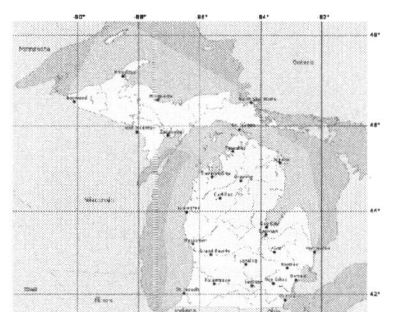
Michigan map, including territorial waters

The state's rivers are generally small, short and shallow, and few are navigable. The principal ones include the Detroit River, St. Marys River, and St. Clair River which connect the Great Lakes; the Au Sable, Cheboygan, and Saginaw, which flow into Lake Huron; the Ontonagon, and Tahquamenon, which flow into Lake Superior; and the St. Joseph, Kalamazoo, Grand, Muskegon, Manistee, and Escanaba, which flow into Lake Michigan. The state has 11,037 inland lakes and 38575 square miles (99910 km^2) of Great Lakes waters and rivers in addition to 1305 square miles (3380 km^2) of inland water. No point in Michigan is more than six miles (10 km) from an inland lake or more than 85 miles (137 km) from one of the Great Lakes.

The state is home to a number of areas maintained by the National Park Service including: Isle Royale National Park, located in Lake Superior, about 30 miles (48 km) southeast of Thunder Bay, Ontario. Other national protected areas in the state include: Keweenaw National Historical Park, Pictured Rocks National Lakeshore, Sleeping Bear Dunes National Lakeshore, Huron National Forest, Manistee National Forest, Hiawatha National Forest, Ottawa National Forest and Father Marquette National Memorial. The largest section of the North Country National Scenic Trail passes through Michigan.

With 78 state parks, 19 state recreation areas, and 6 state forests, Michigan has the largest state park and state forest system of any state. These parks and forests include Holland State Park, Mackinac Island State Park, Au Sable State Forest, and Mackinaw State Forest.

Climate

Detroit, MI
Climate chart (explanation)
J F M A M J J A S O N D
average max. and min. temperatures in °F
precipitation totals in inches
source: Detroit Climate [1]

Metric conversion
J F M A M J J A S O N D
average max. and min. temperatures in °C
precipitation totals in mm

Lansing, MI
Climate chart (explanation)
J F M A M J J A S O N D
average max. and min. temperatures in °F
precipitation totals in inches
source: Lansing Climate [2]

Metric conversion
J F M A M J J A S O N D
average max. and min. temperatures in °C
precipitation totals in mm

Marquette, MI
Climate chart (explanation)
J|F|M|A|M|J|J|A|S|O|N|D
average max. and min. temperatures in °F
precipitation totals in inches
source: Marquette Climate [3]

Metric conversion
J|F|M|A|M|J|J|A|S|O|N|D
average max. and min. temperatures in °C
precipitation totals in mm

Michigan has a continental climate, although there are two distinct regions. The southern and central parts of the Lower Peninsula (south of Saginaw Bay and from the Grand Rapids area southward) have a warmer climate (Koppen climate classification *Dfa*) with hot summers and cold winters. The northern part of Lower Peninsula and the entire Upper Peninsula has a more severe climate (Koppen *Dfb*), with warm, but shorter summers and longer, cold to very cold winters. Some parts of the state average high temperatures below freezing from December through February, and into early March in the far northern parts. During the winter through the middle of February the state is frequently subjected to heavy lake-effect snow. The state averages from 30–40 inches (76–100 cm) of precipitation annually.

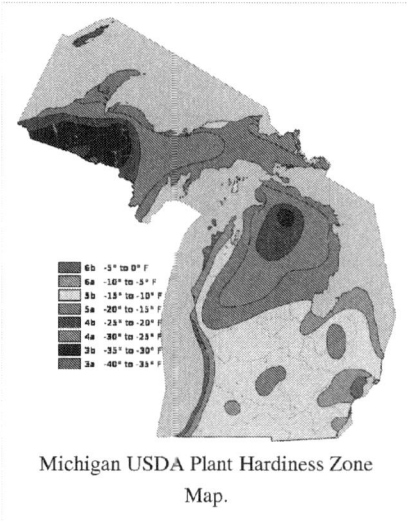

Michigan USDA Plant Hardiness Zone Map.

The entire state averages 30 days of thunderstorm activity per year. These can be severe, especially in the southern part of the state. The state averages 17 tornadoes per year, which are more common in the extreme southern portion of the state. Portions of the southern border have been nearly as vulnerable historically as parts of Tornado Alley. For this reason, many communities in the very southern portions of the state are equipped with tornado sirens to warn residents of approaching tornadoes. Farther north, in the Upper Peninsula, tornadoes are rare.

Monthly Normal High and Low Temperatures For Other Michigan Cities in °F(°C)												
City	Jan	Feb	Mar	Apr	May	Jun	Jul	Aug	Sep	Oct	Nov	Dec
Flint	29/13 (-2/-11)	32/15 (0/-9)	43/24 (6/-4)	56/35 (13/2)	69/45 (21/7)	78/55 (26/13)	82/59 (28/15)	80/57 (27/14)	72/49 (22/9)	60/39 (16/4)	46/30 (8/-1)	34/19 (1/-7)
Grand Rapids	29/16 (-2/-9)	33/17 (1/-8)	43/26 (6/-3)	57/36 (14/2)	70/47 (21/8)	78/56 (26/13)	82/60 (28/16)	80/59 (27/15)	72/51 (22/11)	60/40 (11/4)	46/31 (8/-1)	34/21 (1/-6)
Muskegon	30/17 (-1/-8)	32/18 (0/-8)	42/25 (6/-4)	55/35 (13/2)	67/45 (19/7)	76/54 (24/12)	80/60 (27/16)	78/59 (26/15)	70/51 (21/11)	59/41 (15/5)	46/32 (8/0)	35/23 (2/-5)
Sault Ste. Marie	22/5 (-6/-15)	24/7 (-4/-14)	34/16 (1/-9)	48/29 (9/-2)	63/39 (17/4)	71/46 (22/7)	76/52 (24/11)	74/52 (23/11)	65/45 (18/7)	53/36 (12/2)	39/26 (12/-3)	27/13 (-3/-11)

[4]

Geology

The geological formation of the state is greatly varied. Primary boulders are found over the entire surface of the Upper Peninsula (being principally of primitive origin), while Secondary deposits cover the entire Lower Peninsula. The Upper Peninsula exhibits Lower Silurian sandstones, limestones, copper and iron bearing rocks, corresponding to the Huronian system of Canada. The central portion of the Lower Peninsula contains coal measures and rocks of the Permo-Carboniferous period. Devonian and sub-Carboniferous deposits are scattered over the entire state.

Demographics

See also: Michigan census statistical areas

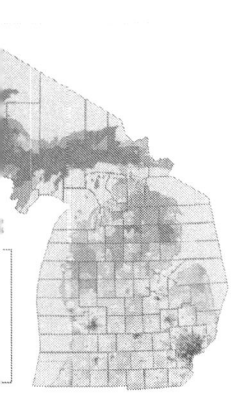
population distribution

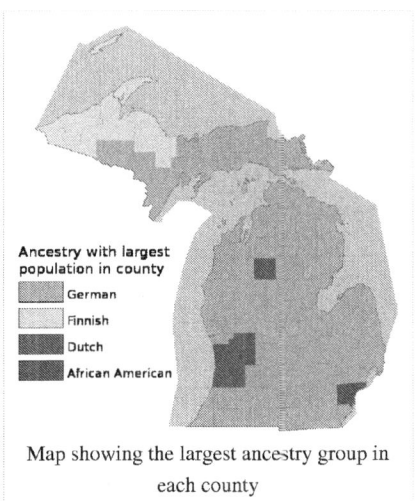
Map showing the largest ancestry group in each county

Historical populations		
Census	Pop.	%±
1800	3757	—
1810	4762	26.8%
1820	7452	56.5%
1830	28004	275.8%
1840	212267	658.0%
1850	397654	87.3%
1860	749113	88.4%
1870	1184059	58.1%
1880	1636937	38.2%
1890	2093890	27.9%
1900	2420982	15.6%
1910	2810173	16.1%
1920	3668412	30.5%
1930	4842325	32.0%
1940	5256106	8.5%
1950	6371766	21.2%
1960	7823194	22.8%
1970	8875083	13.4%

1980	9262078		4.4%
1990	9295297		0.4%
2000	9938444		6.9%
Est. 2008	10045697		1.1%

As of July 1, 2008, Michigan had an estimated population of 10,003,422, an increase of 64,930, or 0.7%, since the year 2000. As of 2000, the state had the eighth-largest population in the Union.

The center of population of Michigan is located in Shiawassee County, in the southeastern corner of the civil township of Bennington, which is located directly north of the village of Morrice.

As of 2005-2007 three-year estimate, the state had a foreign-born population of 610,173, or 6% of the total population. In recent years, the foreign-born population in the state has grown. Michigan has the largest Dutch, Finnish, and Macedonian populations in the United States.

As of the 2006-2008 American Community Survey, the racial composition was as follows:

- White: 79.6% (Non-Hispanic Whites: 77.5%)
- Black or African American: 14.0%
- American Indian: 0.5%
- Asian: 2.3%
- Pacific Islander: <0.1%
- Some other race: 1.6%
- Multiracial: 2.0%
- Hispanic or Latino (of any race): 4.0%

Source:

The five largest reported ancestries in Michigan are German (22.4%), African American (14.0%), Irish (12.0%), English (10.6%), and Polish (9.1%).

The large majority of Michigan's population is Caucasian. Americans of European descent live throughout Michigan and most of Metro Detroit. Large European American groups include those of German, Irish, French, and British ancestry. People of Scandinavian descent, especially those of Finnish ancestry, have a notable presence in the Upper Peninsula. Western Michigan is known for the Dutch heritage of many residents (the highest concentration of any state), especially in metropolitan Grand Rapids. Metro Detroit also has residents of Polish and Irish descent.

Dearborn has become the center of a sizeable Arab community, including many Lebanese who immigrated for jobs in the auto industry in the 1920s. About 300,000 people trace their roots to the Middle East which includes. African Americans, who came to Detroit and other northern cities in the Great Migration of the early 20th century, form a majority of the population of the city of Detroit and of other industrial cities, including Flint and Benton Harbor.

An individual from Michigan is called a "Michigander" or "Michiganian". Also at times, but rarely, a "Michiganite". Residents of the Upper Peninsula are sometimes referred to as "Yoopers" (a phonetic pronunciation of "U.P.ers"), and Upper Peninsula residents sometimes refer to those from the lower as "trolls" (they live below the bridge).

				Demographics of Michigan (csv) [5]	
By race	White	Black	AIAN*	Asian	NHPI*
2000 (total population)	83.05%	14.92%	1.26%	2.10%	0.08%
2000 (Hispanic only)	2.98%	0.22%	0.11%	0.03%	0.01%
2005 (total population)	82.65%	15.05%	1.21%	2.57%	0.08%
2005 (Hispanic only)	3.51%	0.23%	0.11%	0.05%	0.02%
Growth 2000–05 (total population)	1.35%	2.77%	-2.51%	24.24%	12.50%
Growth 2000–05 (non-Hispanic only)	0.66%	2.67%	-2.71%	24.04%	10.70%
Growth 2000–05 (Hispanic only)	19.89%	9.70%	-0.48%	36.87%	20.51%
* AIAN is American Indian or Alaskan Native; NHPI is Native Hawaiian or Pacific Islander					

Religion

The Roman Catholic Church was the only organized religion in Michigan until the 19th century, reflecting the territory's French colonial roots. Detroit's St. Anne's parish, established in 1701, is the second-oldest Catholic parish in the country. French-Canadian Catholics were reduced to a small minority by the influx of Protestants from the United States in the early 19th century. By the mid-19th century, there was a wave of immigration of Catholics from Ireland and, later, from eastern and southern Europe.

Change was rapid in the 19th century. The Lutheran Church was introduced by German and Scandinavian immigrants; Lutheranism is second largest religious denomination in the state. The first Jewish synagogue in the state was Temple Beth El, founded by twelve German Jewish families in Detroit in 1850. Islam was introduced by immigrants from the Near East during the 20th century.

The largest denomination by number of adherents, according to a survey in the year 2000, was the Roman Catholic Church with 2,019,926 parishioners. The largest Protestant denominations were the Lutheran Church–Missouri Synod with 244,231 adherents; followed by the United Methodist Church with 222,269; and the Evangelical Lutheran Church in America with 160,836 adherents. In the same survey, Jewish adherents in the state of Michigan were estimated at 110,000, and Muslims at 80,515.

Economy

See also: List of companies based in Michigan and Economy of metropolitan Detroit

The Bureau of Economic Analysis estimated Michigan's 2004 gross state product at $372 B. Per capita personal income in 2003 was $31,178 and ranked twentieth in the nation. In May 2010, the state's seasonally adjusted unemployment rate was 13.6%, with an actual rate of 12.8% for the month, during a U.S. recession.

\multicolumn{3}{c}{**Top *Fortune* Companies in Michigan for 2009** (ranked by revenues) *with State and U.S. rankings.*}		
State	**Corporation**	**US**
1	General Motors	6
2	Ford	7
3	Dow	38
4	Delphi	121
5	Whirlpool	133
6	Ally	147
7	TRW Automotive	169
8	Lear	195
9	Kellogg	210
10	Penske Automotive	225
11	Masco	277
12	Visteon	282
13	DTE Energy	285
14	Arvin Meritor	346
15	CMS Energy	369
16	Stryker	375
17	Autoliv	376
18	Pulte Homes	393
19	Kelly Services	437
20	BorgWarner	453
21	Auto-Owners	476
22	Steelcase	625

23	Borders Group	639
24	Spartan Stores	751
25	Cooper Standard	814
26	Valassis	809
27	Universal Forest	837
28	Affinia Group	853
29	Hayes-Lemmerz	856
30	American Axle	874
31	Herman Miller	897
32	Perrigo	897

Further information:
List of Michigan companies
Source: Fortune

Some of the major industries/products/services include automobiles, cereal products, pizza, information technology, aerospace, military equipment, copper, iron, and furniture. Michigan is the third leading grower of Christmas trees with 60520 acres (245 km^2) of land dedicated to Christmas tree farming. The beverage Vernors was invented in Michigan in 1866, sharing the title of oldest soft drink with Hires Root Beer. Faygo was founded in Detroit on November 4, 1907. Two of the top four pizza chains were founded in Michigan and are headquartered there: Domino's Pizza by Tom Monaghan and Little Caesars Pizza by Mike Ilitch.

Michigan has experienced economic difficulties brought on by volatile stock market disruptions following the September 11, 2001 attacks. This caused a pension and benefit fund crisis for many American companies, including General Motors, Ford, and Chrysler. Since the early 2000s recession and the September 11, 2001 attacks, GM, Ford, and Chrysler have struggled to overcome the benefit funds crisis which followed an ensuing volatile stock market which had caused a severe underfunding condition in the respective U.S. pension and benefit funds (OPEB). Although manufacturing in the state grew 6.6% from 2001 to 2006, the high speculative price of oil became a factor for the U.S. auto industry during the economic crisis of 2008 impacting industry revenues.

During this economic crisis, President George W. Bush extended loans from the Troubled Assets Relief Program (TARP) funds in order to help the GM and Chrysler bridge the recession. In January 2009, President Barack Obama formed an automotive task force in order to help the industry recover and achieve renewed prosperity for the region. With retiree health care costs a significant issue, General Motors, Ford, and Chrysler reached agreements with the United Auto Workers Union to transfer the liabilities for their respective health care and benefit funds to a 501(c)(9) Voluntary Employee Beneficiary Association (VEBA). In spite of these efforts, the severity of the recession required

Detroit's automakers to take additional steps to restructure, including idling many plants. With the U.S. Treasury extending the necessary debtor in possession financing, Chrysler and GM filed separate 'pre-packaged' Chapter 11 restructurings in May and June 2009 respectively.

Michigan ranks fourth nationally in high tech employment with 568,000 high tech workers, which includes 70,000 in the automotive industry. Michigan typically ranks third or fourth in overall Research & development (R&D) expenditures in the United States. Its research and development, which includes automotive, comprises a higher percentage of the state's overall gross domestic product than for any other U.S. state. The state is an important source of engineering job opportunities. The domestic auto industry accounts directly and indirectly for one of every ten jobs in the U.S.

Michigan ranked second nationally in new corporate facilities and expansions in 2004. From 1997 to 2004, Michigan was listed as the only state to top the 10,000 mark for the number of major new developments; however, the effects of the late 2000s recession have slowed the state's economy. In 2008, Michigan ranked third in a survey among the states for luring new business which measured capital investment and new job creation per one million population. In August 2009, Michigan and Detroit's auto industry received $1.36 B in grants from the U.S. Department of Energy for the manufacture of electric vehicle technologies which is expected to generate 6,800 immediate jobs and employ 40,000 in the state by 2020. From 2007 to 2009, Michigan ranked 3rd in the U.S. for new corporate facilities and expansions.

As leading research institutions, the University of Michigan, Michigan State University, and Wayne State University are important partners in the state's economy and the state's University Research Corridor. Michigan's public universities attract more than $1.5 B in research and development grants each year. The National Superconducting Cyclotron Laboratory is located at Michigan State University. Michigan's workforce is well-educated and highly skilled, making it attractive to companies. It has the third highest number of engineering graduates nationally.

Detroit Metropolitan Airport is one of the nation's most recently expanded and modernized airports with six major runways, and large aircraft maintenance facilities capable of servicing and repairing a Boeing 747. Michigan's schools and colleges rank among the nation's best. The state has maintained its early commitment to public education. The state's infrastructure gives it a competitive edge; Michigan has 38 deep water ports. In 2007, Bank of America announced that it would commit $25 billion to community development in Michigan following its acquisition of LaSalle Bank in Troy.

Taxation

Michigan's personal income tax is set to a flat rate of 4.35%. Some cities impose additional income taxes. Michigan's state sales tax is 6%. Property taxes are assessed on the local level, but every property owner's local assessment contributes six mills (six dollars per thousand dollars of property value) to the statutory State Education Tax. In 2007, Michigan repealed its Single Business Tax (SBT) and replaced it with a Michigan Business Tax (MBT) in order to stimulate job growth by reducing taxes for seventy percent of the businesses in the state. According to the Bureau of Economic Analysis, recent growth in Michigan is 0.1%.

Agriculture

A wide variety of commodity crops, fruits, and vegetables are grown in Michigan, making it second only to California among U.S. states in the diversity of its agriculture. The state has 55,000 farms utilizing 10000000 acres (40000 km^2) of land which sold $6.6 billion worth of products in 2008. The most valuable agricultural product is milk. Leading crops include corn, soybeans, flowers, wheat, sugar beets and potatoes. Livestock in the state included 1 million cattle, 1 million hogs, 78,000 sheep and over 3 million chickens. Livestock products accounted for 38% of the value of agricultural products while crops accounted for the majority.

Michigan is the leading U.S. producer of tart cherries, blueberries, pickling cucumbers, red beans and petunias.

Michigan is a leading grower of fruit in the U.S., including blueberries, cherries, apples, grapes, and peaches. These fruits are mainly grown in West Michigan. Michigan produces wines, beers and a multitude of processed food products. Kellogg's cereal is based out of Battle Creek, Michigan and processes many locally grown foods. Thornapple Valley, Ballpark Franks, Koegel's, and Hebrew National sausage companies are all based in Michigan.

Michigan is home to very fertile land in the Flint/Tri-Cities and "Thumb" areas. Products grown there include corn, sugar beets, navy beans, and soy beans. Sugar beet harvesting usually begins the first of October. It takes the sugar factories about five months to process the 3.7 million tons of sugarbeets into 970 million pounds of pure, white sugar. Michigan's largest sugar refiner, Michigan Sugar Company is the largest east of the Mississippi River and the fourth largest in the nation. Michigan Sugar brand names are Pioneer Sugar and the newly incorporated Big Chief Sugar. Potatoes are grown in Northern Michigan, and corn is dominant in Central Michigan. Michigan State University is dedicated to the study of agriculture.

Tourism

See also: List of National Historic Landmarks in Michigan, List of Registered Historic Places in Michigan, and List of museums in Michigan

Michigan has a thriving tourist industry. Visitors spend $17.5 billion per year in the state, supporting 193,000 tourism jobs. Michigan's tourism website ranks among the busiest in the nation. Destinations draw vacationers, hunters, and nature enthusiasts from across the United States and Canada. Michigan is fifty percent forest land, much of it quite remote. The forests, lakes and thousands of miles of beaches are top attractions. Event tourism draws large numbers to occasions like the Tulip Time Festival and the National Cherry Festival.

The Grand Hotel on Mackinac Island is a classic image of Michigan tourism.

In 2006, the Michigan State Board of Education mandated that all public schools in the state hold their first day of school after the Labor Day holiday, in accordance with the new Post Labor Day School law. A survey found that 70% of all tourism business comes directly from Michigan residents, and the Michigan Hotel, Motel, & Resort Association claimed that the shorter summer in between school years cut into the annual tourism season in the state.

Tourism in metropolitan Detroit draws visitors to leading attractions, particularly The Henry Ford, the Detroit Institute of Arts, and the Detroit Zoo, and to sports in Detroit. Other museums include the Detroit Historical Museum, the Charles H. Wright Museum of African American History, museums in the Cranbrook Educational Community, and the Arab American National Museum. The metro area offers four major casinos, MGM Grand Detroit, Greektown, Motor City, and Caesars Windsor in Windsor, Ontario, Canada; moreover, Detroit is the largest American city and metropolitan region to offer casino resorts.

Hunting and fishing are significant industries in the state. Charter boats are based in many Great Lakes cities to fish for salmon, trout, walleye and perch. Michigan ranks first in the nation in licensed hunters (over one million) who contribute $2 billion annually to its economy. Over three-quarters of a million hunters participate in white-tailed deer season alone. Many school districts in rural areas of Michigan cancel school on the opening day of firearm deer season, because of attendance concerns.

Michigan's Department of Natural Resources manages the largest dedicated state forest system in the nation. The forest products industry and recreational users contribute $12 billion and 200,000 associated jobs annually to the state's economy. Public hiking and hunting access has also been secured in extensive commercial forests. The state has highest number of golf courses and registered snowmobiles in the nation.

The state has numerous historical markers, which can themselves become the center of a tour. The Great Lakes Circle Tour is a designated scenic road system connecting all of the Great Lakes and the St. Lawrence River.

With its position in relation to the Great Lakes and the countless ships that have foundered over the many years in which they have been used as a transport route for people and bulk cargo, Michigan is a world-class scuba diving destination. The Michigan Underwater Preserves are 11 underwater areas where wrecks are protected for the benefit of sport divers.

Transportation

Michigan has nine international crossings with Ontario, Canada:

Mackinac Bridge

- Ambassador Bridge, North America's busiest international border crossing the Detroit River
- Blue Water Bridge, a twin-span bridge (Port Huron, Michigan and Point Edward, Ontario, but the larger city of Sarnia, Ontario is usually referred to on the Canadian side.)
- Blue Water Ferry (Marine City, Michigan and Sombra, Ontario)
- Canadian Pacific Railway tunnel.
- Detroit–Windsor Truck Ferry (Detroit, Michigan and Windsor, Ontario)
- Detroit–Windsor Tunnel.
- International Bridge (Sault Ste. Marie, Michigan and Sault Ste. Marie, Ontario)
- St. Clair River Railway Tunnel (Port Huron, Michigan and Sarnia, Ontario)
- Walpole Island Ferry (Algonac, Michigan and Walpole Island First Nation, Ontario

A second international bridge is currently under development between Detroit, Michigan and Windsor, Ontario.

Railroads

See also: List of Michigan railroads and History of railroads in Michigan

Michigan is served by four Class I railroads: the Canadian National Railway, the Canadian Pacific Railway, CSX Transportation, and the Norfolk Southern Railway. These are augmented by several dozen short line railroads. The vast majority of rail service in Michigan is devoted to freight, with Amtrak and various scenic railroads the exceptions.

Main article: Michigan Services

Amtrak passenger rail services the state, connecting many southern and western Michigan cities to Chicago, Illinois. There are plans for commuter rail for Detroit and its suburbs (see SEMCOG Commuter Rail).

Roadways

See also: Michigan Highway System

Interstate 75 is the main thoroughfare between Detroit, Flint, and Saginaw extending north to Sault Sainte Marie and providing access to Sault Sainte Marie, Ontario. The expressway crosses the Mackinac Bridge between the Lower and Upper Peninsulas. Branching highways include I-275 and I-375 in Detroit; I-475 in Flint; and I-675 in Saginaw.

Welcome sign.

Interstate 69 enters the state near the Michigan-Ohio-Indiana border, and it extends to Port Huron and provides access to the Blue Water Bridge crossing into Sarnia, Ontario.

Interstate 94 enters the western end of the state at the Indiana border, and it travels east to Detroit and then northeast to Port Huron and ties in with I-69. I-194 branches off from this freeway in Battle Creek. I-94 is the main artery between Chicago, Illinois and Detroit.

Interstate 96 runs east–west between Detroit and Muskegon. I-496 loops through Lansing. I-196 branches off from this freeway at Grand Rapids and connects to I-94 near Benton Harbor. I-696 branches off from this freeway at Novi and connects to I-94 near St Clair Shores.

U.S. Route 2 enters Michigan at the city of Ironwood and runs east to the town of Crystal Falls, where it turns south and briefly re-enters Wisconsin northwest of Florence. It re-enters Michigan north of Iron Mountain and continues through the Upper Peninsula of Michigan to the cities of Escanaba, Manistique, and St. Ignace. Along the way, it cuts through the Ottawa and Hiawatha National Forests and follows the northern shore of Lake Michigan. Its eastern terminus lies at exit 344 of I-75, just north of the Mackinac Bridge. This is generally regarded as the main route through the Upper Peninsula, although some prefer to travel on M-28 as it tends to save time (U.S. 2 hugs the Lake Michigan shoreline for much of its length.)

Major bridges include the Ambassador Bridge, Blue Water Bridge, Mackinac Bridge, and International Bridge. Michigan also has the Detroit-Windsor Tunnel crossing into Canada.

Airports

See also: List of airports in Michigan

The Detroit Metropolitan Wayne County Airport is Michigan's busiest airport, followed by the Gerald R. Ford International Airport in Grand Rapids.

Important cities and townships

Further information: List of cities, villages, and townships in Michigan

The largest municipalities in Michigan are (according to 2009 census estimates):

The Grand Rapids skyline centered on the Grand River.

A Lansing sunset

Downtown Flint as seen from the Flint River.

The Ann Arbor skyline as seen from Michigan Stadium.

Rank	City	Population
1	Detroit	910,920
2	Grand Rapids	193,710
3	Warren	133,872
4	Sterling Heights	127,176
5	Lansing	113,810
6	Ann Arbor	112,852
7	Flint	111,475
8	Clinton Township	95,990
9	Livonia	89,282
10	Dearborn	84,575

Map showing largest Michigan municipalities.

Other important cities include:

- Battle Creek ("Cereal City U.S.A.", world headquarters of Kellogg Company)
- Benton Harbor / St. Joseph (headquarters of Whirlpool Corporation)
- East Lansing (home of Michigan State University)
- Big Rapids (home of Ferris State University)
- Holland (home of Tulip Time, the largest tulip festival in the U.S.)
- Jackson (headquarters of CMS Energy)
- Kalamazoo (Largest city in southwest Michigan and home to Western Michigan University)
- Manistee (home to the world's largest salt plant, owned by Morton Salt)
- Marquette (largest city in the Upper Peninsula with 19,661 people and home of Northern Michigan University)
- Midland (headquarters of the Dow Chemical Company and the Dow Corning Corporation)
- Mount Pleasant (home of Central Michigan University)
- Muskegon (largest Michigan city on Lake Michigan)
- Pontiac (major automobile manufacturing center, and home of the Pontiac Silverdome)
- Port Huron (major international crossing and home of the Blue Water Bridge)
- Saginaw (the largest of the Tri-Cities, which also consist of Bay City and Midland, and home to Saginaw Valley State University)
- Sault Ste. Marie (home of the Soo Locks and Sault Ste. Marie International Bridge)
- Traverse City ("Cherry Capital of the World", making Michigan the country's largest producer of cherries)
- Ypsilanti (home of Eastern Michigan University)

Half of the wealthiest communities in the state are located in Oakland County, just north of Detroit. Another wealthy community is located just east of the city, in Grosse Pointe. Only three of these cities are located outside of Metro Detroit. The city of Detroit itself, with a per capita income of $14,717, ranks 517th on the list of Michigan locations by per capita income. Benton Harbor is the poorest city in Michigan, with a per capita income of $8,965, while Barton Hills is the richest with a per capita income of $110,683.

Education

See also: List of colleges and universities in Michigan and List of high schools in Michigan

Michigan's education system provides services to 1.6 million K-12 students in public schools. More than 124,000 students attend private schools and an uncounted number are homeschooled under certain legal requirements. The public school system has a $14.5 billion budget in 2008-2009. Michigan has a number of public universities spread throughout the state and a numerous private colleges as well. Michigan State University has one of the largest enrollments of any U.S. school. Michigan State and University of Michigan are leading research institutions.

Professional sports

Main article: List of Michigan professional sports teams

Michigan's major-league sports teams include: Detroit Tigers baseball team, Detroit Lions football team, Detroit Red Wings ice hockey team, and the Detroit Pistons men's basketball team.

The Pistons played at Detroit's Cobo Arena until 1978 and at the Pontiac Silverdome until 1988 when they moved into the Palace of Auburn Hills. The Detroit Lions played at Tiger Stadium in Detroit until 1974, then moved to the Pontiac Silverdome where they played for 27 years between 1975-2002 before moving to Ford Field in Detroit in 2002. The Detroit Tigers played at Tiger Stadium (Detroit) (formerly known as Navin Field and Briggs Stadium) from 1912 to 1999. In 2000 they moved to Comerica Park. The Red Wings played at Olympia Stadium before moving to Joe Louis Arena in 1979.

Thirteen-time Grand Slam champion Serena Williams was born in Saginaw. The Michigan International Speedway is the site of NASCAR races and Detroit was formerly the site of a Grand Prix race. Michigan is home to one of the major canoeing marathons: the 120-mile (190 km) Au Sable River Canoe Marathon. Professional hockey got its start in Houghton, when the Portage Lakers were formed.

State symbols and nicknames

Michigan is, by tradition, known as "The Wolverine State," and the University of Michigan takes the wolverine as its mascot. The association is well and long established: for example, many Detroiters volunteered to fight during the American Civil War and George Armstrong Custer, who led the Michigan Brigade, called them the "Wolverines". The origins of this association are obscure; it may derive from a busy trade in wolverine furs in Sault Ste. Marie in the 18th century or may recall a disparagement intended to compare early settlers in Michigan with the vicious mammal. Wolverines are, however, extremely rare in Michigan. A sighting in February 2004 near Ubly was the first confirmed sighting in Michigan in 200 years. The animal was found dead in 2010.

- State nicknames: *Wolverine State, Great Lakes State, Mitten State, Water-Winter Wonderland*
- State motto: *Si quaeris peninsulam amoenam circumspice* (Latin: If you seek a pleasant peninsula, look about you) adopted in 1835 on the coat-of-arms, but never as an official 'motto'. This is a paraphrase of the epitaph of British architect Sir Christopher Wren about his masterpiece, St. Paul's Cathedral.
- State song: *My Michigan* (official since 1937, but disputed amongst residents), *Michigan, My Michigan* (Unofficial State Song, since the civil war)
- State bird: American Robin (since 1931)
- State animal: Wolverine (traditional)
- State game animal: White-tailed deer (since 1997)
- State fish: Brook trout (since 1965)
- State reptile: Painted Turtle (since 1995)
- State fossil: Mastodon (since 2000)
- State flower: Apple blossom (adopted in 1897, official in 1997)
- State wildflower: Dwarf Lake Iris (since 1998). Known as *Iris lacustris*, it is a federally listed threatened species.
- State tree: White pine (since 1955)
- State stone: Petoskey stone (since 1965). It is composed of fossilized coral (*Hexagonaria pericarnata*) from long ago when the middle of the continent was covered with a shallow sea.
- State gem: Isle Royale greenstone (since 1973). Also called *chlorastrolite* (literally "green star stone"), the mineral is found on Isle Royale and the Keweenaw peninsula.
- State Quarter: U.S. coin issued in 2004 with the Michigan motto "Great Lake State."
- State soil: Kalkaska Sand (since 1990), ranges in color from black to yellowish brown, covers nearly 1000000-acre (4000 km^2) in 29 counties.

Sister states

- Shiga Prefecture, Japan
- Sichuan Province, Peoples Republic of China

See also

- Outline of Michigan
- Index of Michigan-related articles
- USS Michigan

Further reading

- Bald, F. Clever, *Michigan in Four Centuries* (1961)/
- Browne, William P. and - Kenneth VerBurg. *Michigan Politics & Government: Facing Change in a Complex State* University of Nebraska Press. 1995.
- Bureau of Business Research, Wayne State U. *Michigan Statistical Abstract* (1987).
- Clarke Historical Library, Central Michigan University, Bibliographies for Michigan by region, counties, etc. [6].
- Dunbar, Willis F. and George S. May. *Michigan: A History of the Wolverine State* (1995) excerpt and text search [7]
- Michigan, State of. *Michigan Manual* (annual), elaborate detail on state government.
- Press, Charles et al., *Michigan Political Atlas* (1984).
- Public Sector Consultants. *Michigan in Brief. An Issues Handbook* (annual)
- Rich, Wilbur. *Coleman Young and Detroit Politics: From Social Activist to Power Broker* (Wayne State University Press, 1988).
- Rubenstein, Bruce A. and Lawrence E. Ziewacz. *Michigan: A History of the Great Lakes State.* (2nd ed. 2008)
- Sisson, Richard, Ed. *The American Midwest: An Interpretive Encyclopedia* (2006)
- Weeks, George, *Stewards of the State: The Governors of Michigan* (Historical Society of Michigan, 1987).

External links

- State of Michigan government website [8]
- Energy Data & Statistics for Michigan [9]
- Info Michigan, detailed information on 630 cities [10]
- Michigan Historic Markers [11]
- Michigan History Magazine [12]
- Michigan Lighthouse Chronology - Clark Historical Library [13]
- Michigan State Guide from the Library of Congress [14]
- Michigan Official Travel Site [15]
- Michigan travel guide from Wikitravel
- Michigan [16] at the Open Directory Project
- Michigan State Fact Sheet [17] from the U.S. Department of Agriculture
- Michigan Underwater Preserves Council [18]
- The Michigan Municipal League [19]
- USGS real-time, geographic, and other scientific resources of Michigan [20]

Bold Faced States/Provinces bound Michigan completely over water.

Bold Italicized States bound Michigan partially over water.

None of Michigan's neighbors border them completely over land. Even Indiana and Ohio have small portions of border that is over one of the Great Lakes, Lake Michigan (Indiana) and Lake Erie (Ohio).

Wisconsin's border with Michigan is mainly over water except for most of their border with the Upper Peninsula, which is over land and to the southwest.

1. REDIRECT Template:Navboxes

Geographical coordinates: 44°20′N 85°35′W

frr:Michigan pnb:مشیگن

History

History of Michigan

The **History of Michigan** is divided into the following articles.

See also Timeline of Michigan history.

Main article: Michigan

Aerial photo of Soo Locks and International Bridge displaying the historic relationships Michigan has with the Great Lakes and Canada.

Before 1776

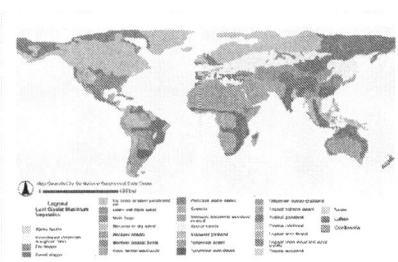

Map of last glacial period with Michigan and Great Lakes Basin entirely covered by an ice sheet.

Thousands of years before the arrival of the first Europeans, several indigenous tribes lived in what is today the state of Michigan. They included the Ojibwa, Menominee, Miami, Ottawa, and Potawatomi, who were part of the Algonquian family of Amerindians, as well as the Wyandot, who were from the Iroquoian family and lived in the area of present-day Detroit. It is estimated that the native population at the time the first European arrived was 15,000.

The first white explorer to visit Michigan was the Frenchman Étienne Brûlé in 1620, who began his expedition from Quebec City on the orders of Samuel de Champlain and traveled as far as the Upper Peninsula. Afterward, the area became part of Louisiana, one of the large colonial provinces of New France. The first permanent European settlement in Michigan was founded in 1668 at Sault Ste. Marie by Jacques Marquette, a French missionary.

The French built several trading posts, forts, and villages in Michigan during the late 17th century. Among them, the most important was Fort Pontchartrain du Détroit, established by Antoine de Lamothe Cadillac. This grew to become Detroit. Up until this time, French activities in the region were limited to hunting, trapping, trading with and the conversion of local Indians, and some limited subsistence agriculture. By 1760, the Michigan countryside had only a few hundred white inhabitants.

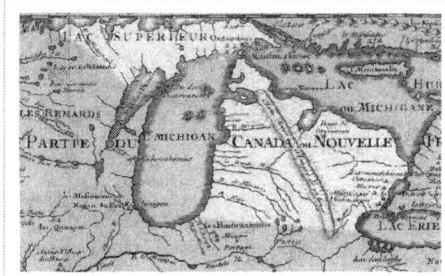

Michigan in 1718, Guillaume de L'Isle map, approximate state area highlighted.

Territorial disputes between French and British colonists helped start the French and Indian War as part of the larger Seven Years' War, which took place from 1754 to 1763 and resulted in the defeat of France. As part of the Treaty of Paris, the French ceded all of their North American colonies east of the Mississippi River to Britain. Thus the future Michigan was handed over to the British. In 1774, the area was made part of Quebec. It continued to be sparsely populated. Regional growth proceeded slowly because the British were more interested in the fur trade and peace with the natives than in settlement of the area.

From 1776 to 1837

During the American Revolutionary War, the local European population, who were primarily American colonists that supported independence, rebelled against Britain. The British, with the help of local tribes, continually attacked American settlements in the region starting in 1776 and conquered Detroit. In 1781, Spanish raiders led by a French Captain Eugene Poure travelled by river and overland from St Louis, liberated British-held Fort St Joseph, and handed authority over the settlement to the Americans the following day. The war ended with the signing of the Treaty of Paris in 1783, and Michigan passed into the control of the newly formed United States of America. In 1787, the region became part of the Northwest Territory. The British, however, continued to occupy Detroit and other fortifications and did not definitively leave the area until after the implementation of the Jay Treaty in 1796.

Unfinished contemporaneous painting of the American diplomatic negotiators of the Treaty of Paris which brought official conclusion to the Revolutionary War and gave possession of Michigan and other territory to the new United States.

The land which is now Michigan was made part of Indiana Territory in 1800. Most was declared as Michigan Territory in 1805, including all of the Lower Peninsula. During the War of 1812, British forces from Canada captured Detroit and Fort Mackinac early on, giving them a strategic advantage and encouraging native revolt against the United States. American troops retook Detroit in 1813 and Fort Mackinac was returned to the Americans at the end of the war in 1815.

Over the 1810s, the indigenous Ojibwa, Ottawa, and Potawatomi tribes increasingly decided to oppose white settlement and sided with the British against the U.S. government.

After their defeat in the War of 1812, the tribes were forced to sell all of their land claims to the US federal government by the Treaty of Saginaw and the Treaty of Chicago. After the war, the government built forts in some of the northwest territory, such as at Sault Ste. Marie. In the 1820s the US government assigned Indian agents to work with the tribes, including arranging land cessions and relocation. They forced most of the Native Americans to relocate from Michigan to Indian reservations further west.

During the 1820s, the population of Michigan Territory grew rapidly, largely because of the opening of the Erie Canal in 1825. Its connection of the navigable waters of the middle Great Lakes to those of the Atlantic Ocean dramatically sped up transportation between the eastern states and the less-inhabited western territories. The canal created new possibilities for transport of produce and goods to market, as well as easing passage of migrants to the west.

Michigan's oldest university, the University of Michigan was founded in Detroit in 1817 and was later moved to its present location in Ann Arbor. The state's oldest cultural instititon, the Historical Society of Michigan, was established by territorial governor Lewis Cass and explorer Henry Schoolcraft in 1828.

Rising settlement prompted the elevation of Michigan Territory to that of the present-day state. In 1835, the federal government enacted a law that would have created a State of Michigan. A territorial dispute with Ohio over the Toledo Strip, a stretch of land including the city of Toledo, delayed the final accession of statehood. The disputed zone became part of Ohio by the order of a revised bill passed by the U.S. Congress and signed into law by President Andrew Jackson which also gave compensation to Michigan in the form of control of the Upper Peninsula. On January 26, 1837, Michigan became the 26th state of the Union.

From 1837 to 1900

During the early 1840s, large deposits of copper and iron ores were discovered on the Upper Peninsula.

Michigan actively participated in the American Civil War sending thousands of volunteers. After the war, the local economy became more varied and began to prosper economically. During the 1870s, the lumber industry, dairy farming and diversified industry grew rapidly in the state. The population doubled between 1870 and 1890.

Toward the end of the century, the state government established a state school system on the German model, with public schools, high schools, normal schools or colleges for training teachers of lower grades, and colleges for classical academic studies and professors. It dedicated more funds to public education than did any other state in the nation. Within a few years, it established four-year curriculums at its normal colleges, and was the first state to establish a full college program for them.

Railroads have been vital in the history of the population and trade of rough and finished goods in the state of Michigan. While some coastal settlements had previously existed, the population, commercial, and industrial growth of the state further bloomed with the establishment of the railroad.

1900 to 1941

During the early 20th century, manufacturing industries became the main source of revenue for Michigan – in large part, because of the automobile. In 1899, the Olds Motor Vehicle Company opened a factory in Detroit. In 1903, Ford Motor Company was also founded there. With the mass production of the Ford Model T, Detroit became the world capital of the auto industry. General Motors is based in Detroit, Chrysler is located in Rochester Hills, and Ford is headquartered in nearby Dearborn. Both corporations constructed large industrial complexes in the Detroit metropolitan area, exemplified by the River Rouge Plant, which have made Michigan a national leader in manufacturing since the 1910s. This industrial base produced greatly during World War I, filling a huge demand for military vehicles.

Photo of workers occupying a General Motors car body factory during the Flint Sit-Down Strike which spurred the organization of unions in the U.S. auto industry.

Jackson was home to one of the first car industry developments. Even before Detroit began building cars on assembly lines, Jackson was busy making parts for cars and putting them together in 1901. By 1910, the auto industry became Jackson's main industry. Over twenty different cars were once made in Jackson. Including: Reeves, Jaxon, Jackson, CarterCar, Orlo, Whiting, Butcher and Gage, Buick, Janney, Globe, Steel Swallow, C.V.I., Imperial, Ames-Dean, Cutting, Standard Electric, Duck, Briscoe, Argo, Hollier, Hackett, Marion-Handly, Gem, Earl, Wolverine, and Kaiser-Darrin. Today the auto industry remains one of the largest employers of skilled machine operators in Jackson County.

With the expansion of industry, hundreds of thousands of migrants from the South and immigrants from eastern and southern Europe were attracted to Detroit. In a short time, it became the fourth largest city in the country - housing shortages persisted for years even as new housing was developed throughout the city. Ethnic immigrant enclaves rapidly developed where churches, bakeries and businesses supported unique communities. A guide to the city written in the 1930s noted that there were students speaking more than 35 languages in the public schools. Ethnic festivals were a regular part of the city's culture. At the same time, such rapid social change created an environment in which the second Ku Klux Klan recruited members in the city. Their influence was at a peak in 1925, but membership fell quickly after that.

The Great Depression caused severe economic hardship in Michigan. Thousands of auto industry workers were dismissed along with other workers from several sectors of the state economy. The financial suffering was aggravated by the fact that remaining copper reserves in the state lay deep underground. With the discovery of copper finds in other states located in less deep rock layers, local mining fell sharply and resulted in unemployment for thousands of miners. The federal government took several measures to try to diminish the negative effects. It created the Civilian Conservation Corps, a work relief program that started hiring thousands of unemployed young men for jobs like maintenance and cleaning. The Works Progress Administration was another federal agency which hired more than 500,000 unemployed people in Michigan alone to construct major public works such as roads, buildings, and dams.

During this time, United Auto Workers was founded to represent automotive industry employees. This labor union pressured Michigan auto companies to hire for contract only workers who were union members and wanted to handle negotiations between managers and workers. Ford and General Motors became the main targets of the UAW, and continuous strikes, the most important of which was the Flint Sit-Down Strike, forced both companies to recognize the existence of the union. Today, the UAW is one of the largest unions in the United States and has represented all of the employed workers of domestic automobile companies since 1941.

After 1941

The entry of the United States into World War II the same year ended the economic contraction in Michigan. Wartime required the large-scale production of weapons and military vehicles, leading to a massive number of new jobs being filled. After the end of the war, both the automotive and copper mining industries recovered.

Starting during WWI, the Great Migration fueled the movement of thousands of African-Americans from the South to industrial jobs in Michigan and, especially, Detroit. Migration of white southerners to the city increased the volatility of change. Population increases continued with industrial expansion during WWII and afterward. African Americans contributed to a new vibrant urban culture, with expansion of new music, food and culture.

Gerald Ford, a politician from Grand Rapids who was elected to the House of Representatives thirteen times and also served as House Minority Leader and then Vice President, became the 38th President of the United States after the resignation of Richard Nixon.

The postwar years were initially a prosperous time for industrial workers, who achieved middle-class livelihoods. These were the years of the creation and popularity of Motown Records. By late mid-century, however, deindustrialization and restructuring cost many jobs. The economy suffered and the city postponed needed changes. Neglect of social problems and urban decline fed racial conflicts. In 1967 the 12th St. Riot erupted, lasting eight days, causing 25 million dollars in damages, and resulting in 43 deaths. The violence caused many people to leave the city who could, to avoid future problems.

The 1973 Oil Crisis caused economic recession in the United States and greatly affected the Michigan economy. Afterward, automobile companies in the United States faced greater multinational competition, especially from Japan. As a consequence, domestic auto makers enacted cost-cutting measures to remain competitive at home and abroad. Unemployment rates rose dramatically in the state.

Throughout the 1970s, Michigan possessed the highest unemployment rate of any U.S. state. Large spending cuts to education and public health were repeatedly made in an attempt to reduce growing state budget deficits. A strengthening of the auto industry and an increase in tax revenue stabilized government and household finances in the 1980s. Increasing competition by Japanese and South Korean auto companies continues to challenge the state economy, which depends heavily on the automobile industry. Since the late 1980s, the government of Michigan has actively sought to attract new industries, thus reducing economic reliance on a single sector.

Further reading

- Bald, F. Clever, *Michigan in Four Centuries* (1961)
- Browne, William P. and - Kenneth VerBurg. *Michigan Politics & Government: Facing Change in a Complex State* University of Nebraska Press. 1995.
- Bureau of Business Research, Wayne State U. *Michigan Statistical Abstract* (1987).
- Clarke Historical Library, Central Michigan University, Bibliographies for Michigan by region, counties, etc. [6].
- Dunbar, Willis F. and George S. May. *Michigan: A History of the Wolverine State* (1995) excerpt and text search [7]
- Michigan, State of. *Michigan Manual* (annual), elaborate detail on state government.
- *Michigan Historical Review* Central Michigan University (quarterly).
- Nolan, Alan T. *The Iron Brigade: A Military History* (1994), famous Civil War combat unit
- Press, Charles et al., *Michigan Political Atlas* (1984).
- Public Sector Consultants. *Michigan in Brief. An Issues Handbook* (annual)
- Rich, Wilbur. *Coleman Young and Detroit Politics: From Social Activist to Power Broker* (Wayne State University Press, 1988).
- Rubenstein, Bruce A. and Lawrence E. Ziewacz. *Michigan: A History of the Great Lakes State.* (2002)
- Sisson, Richard, Ed. *The American Midwest: An Interpretive Encyclopedia* (2006)
- Trap. Paul, and Larry Wagenaar. *Michigan History Directory of Historical Societies, Museums, Archives, Historic Sites, Agencies and Commissions* (12th Ed. 2008)
- Weeks, George, *Stewards of the State: The Governors of Michigan* (Historical Society of Michigan, 1987).

See also

Main article: Historical outline of Michigan

- Algonquian peoples
- European colonization of the Americas
- History of Detroit
- History of Ford Motor Company
- History of General Motors
- History of railroads in Michigan

- History of the Midwestern United States
- International Boundary Waters Treaty
- Inland Northern American English
- Northwest Ordinance
- List of Michigan county name etymologies
- List of museums in Michigan
- Sixty Years' War
- Timeline of Michigan history
- Timeline of the Toledo Strip/War
- War of 1812

External links

- Historical Society of Michigan [1]
- Official State of Michigan History, Arts & Libraries homepage (MHAL) [2]

Cyrus G. Luce

Cyrus Luce	
21ˢᵗ Governor of Michigan	
In office January 1, 1887 – January 1, 1891	
Lieutenant	1. James H. MacDonald 2. William Ball
Preceded by	Russell Alger
Succeeded by	Edwin B. Winans
Born	July 2, 1824 Windsor, Ohio
Died	March 18, 1905 (aged 80) Coldwater, Michigan
Political party	Republican
Spouse(s)	1. Julia A. Dickinson 2. Mary Thompson
Religion	Presbyterian

Cyrus Gray Luce (July 2, 1824–March 18, 1905) was the 21st Governor of the U.S. state of Michigan.

Early life in Ohio and Indiana

Luce was born in Windsor, Ashtabula County, Ohio. His father, a veteran of the War of 1812 from Tolland, Connecticut, settled in the Connecticut Western Reserve after the war. When he was twelve years old, Cyrus moved west with his family to Steuben County, Indiana. After leaving school at age 17, Luce worked from 1841 until 1848 in a woolen mill, carding wool and dressing the unfinished cloth for sale.

In 1848, he was a Whig Party candidate for the Indiana House of Representatives for the district including Steuben and DeKalb counties. He lost a close election, and in the same year he purchased 80 acres (320000 m^2) of uncultivated land near Gilead, Michigan in Branch County not far from the Indiana state line.

Life and Politics in Michigan

Luce cleared the land for farming and in 1849 married Julia A. Dickinson of Gilead. Over time, he expanded his landholdings with additional purchases. He became an active member of the Grange in 1874, and remained active in the organization for many years afterwards.

In 1852, he was elected to represent Gilead Township on the Branch County Board of Supervisors. In 1854, he was elected as a candidate of the newly-formed Republican party to the Michigan State House of Representatives, serving from 1855-1856. He was elected Branch County Treasurer in 1858 and again in 1860. In 1864, he was named to fill a seat in the Michigan Senate and was re-elected in 1866. In July, 1879, Luce was appointed State Oil Inspector by Governor Charles Croswell, and re-appointed by Gov. David Jerome in 1881.

His first wife Julia died in August 1882, and Luce married Mary Thompson of Bronson, Michigan in November 1883.

Running as a Republican party candidate, Luce was elected Governor of Michigan in November 1886, defeating George L. Yaple, taking office on January 1, 1887. He was reelected in 1888 and served two two-year terms. During his tenure, the position of state game warden was established and a local liquor option law was sanctioned.

Death and legacy

Luce died at the age of 80 in Coldwater, Michigan, and is buried in Oak Grove Cemetery adjacent to that municipality.

Luce County, in the Upper Peninsula of Michigan, is named for him. He was the last governor of the state to have a county named in his honor. His administration was marked by rapid population growth and development in northern Michigan, led by the lumber industry. A state landmark, the Grand Hotel on Mackinac Island, was built in 1887 during his administration.

External links

- Political Graveyard [1]
- Find A Grave [2]
- Memorial Library [3]
- Michigan Historical Marker [4]
- National Governors Association [5]

Geography

Upper Peninsula of Michigan

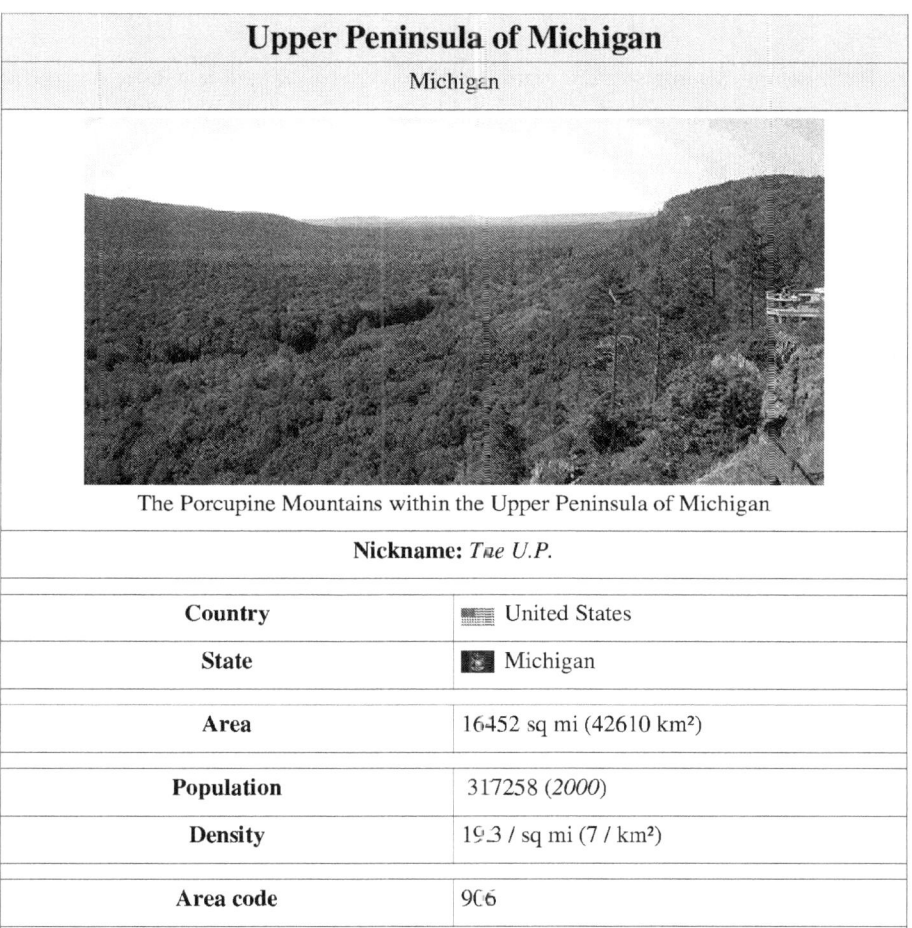

Upper Peninsula of Michigan	
Michigan	
The Porcupine Mountains within the Upper Peninsula of Michigan	
Nickname: *The U.P.*	
Country	United States
State	Michigan
Area	16452 sq mi (42610 km²)
Population	317258 (*2000*)
Density	19.3 / sq mi (7 / km²)
Area code	906

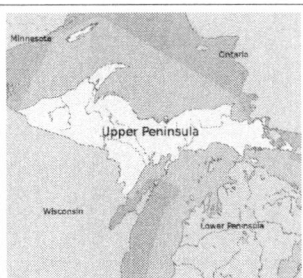

The Upper Peninsula is bordered by the Lower Peninsula, Wisconsin, Minnesota, and Ontario

The **Upper Peninsula of Michigan** is the northern of the two major land masses that make up the U.S. state of Michigan. It is commonly referred to as the **Upper Peninsula**, **the U.P.**, or **Upper Michigan**. More casually it is known as the land "above the Bridge" (above the Mackinac Bridge linking the two peninsulas). It is bounded on the north by Lake Superior, on the east by the St. Mary's River, on the southeast by Lake Michigan and Lake Huron, and on the southwest by Wisconsin.

The Upper Peninsula contains almost one-fourth of the land area of Michigan but just three percent of its total population. Residents are frequently called Yoopers (derived from "U.P.-ers") and have a strong regional identity. It includes the only counties in the United States where a plurality of residents claim Finnish ancestry. Large numbers of Finnish, Swedish, Danish and Norwegian emigrants came to the Upper Peninsula, especially the Keweenaw Peninsula, to work in the mines, and they stayed on and prospered even after the copper mines closed.

Ordered by size, the peninsula's largest cities are Marquette, Sault Ste. Marie, Escanaba, Menominee, Iron Mountain, and Houghton. The land and climate are not very suitable for agriculture because of the long harsh winters. The economy has been based on logging, mining and tourism. Most mines have closed since the "golden age" from 1890 to 1920. The land is heavily forested and logging remains a major industry.

History

Main articles: Timeline of Michigan history and History of Michigan

The first known inhabitants of the Upper Peninsula were tribes speaking Algonquian languages. They arrived roughly around AD 800 and subsisted chiefly from fishing. Early tribes included the Menominee, Nocquet, and the Mishinimaki. Étienne Brûlé of France was probably the first European to visit the peninsula, crossing the St. Marys River around 1620 in search of a route to the Far East.

French colonists laid claim to the land in the 17th century, establishing missions and fur trading posts such as Sault Ste. Marie and St. Ignace. Following the end of the French and Indian War (part of the Seven Years' War) in 1763, the territory was ceded to Great Britain.

American Indian tribes formerly allied with the French were dissatisfied with the British occupation, which brought new territorial policies. Whereas the French cultivated alliances among the Indians, the

British postwar approach was to treat the tribes as conquered peoples. In 1763 tribes united in Pontiac's Rebellion to try to drive the British from the area. American Indians captured Fort Michilimackinac, near present-day Mackinaw City, Michigan, then the principal fort of the British in the Michilimackinac region, as well as others and killed hundreds of British. In 1764 they began negotiations with the British which resulted in temporary peace and changes in objectionable British policies.

Although the Upper Peninsula nominally became United States territory with the 1783 Treaty of Paris, the British did not give up control until 1797 under terms of the Jay Treaty. As an American territory, the Upper Peninsula was still dominated by the fur trade. John Jacob Astor founded the American Fur Company on Mackinac Island in 1808; however, the industry began to decline in the 1830s as beaver and other game were overhunted.

When the Michigan Territory was first established in 1805, it included only the Lower Peninsula and the eastern portion of the Upper Peninsula. In 1819 the territory was expanded to include the remainder of the Upper Peninsula, all of Wisconsin, and part of Minnesota (previously included in the Indiana and Illinois Territories). When Michigan was preparing for statehood in the 1830s, the boundaries proposed corresponded to the original territorial boundaries, with some proposals even leaving the Upper Peninsula out entirely. Meanwhile, the territory was involved in a border dispute with the state of Ohio in a conflict known as the Toledo War.

The people of Michigan approved a constitution in May 1835 and elected state officials in late autumn 1835. Although the state government was not yet recognized by the United States Congress, the territorial government effectively ceased to exist. A constitutional convention of the state legislature refused a compromise to accept the full Upper Peninsula in exchange for ceding the Toledo Strip to Ohio. A second convention, hastily convened by Governor Stevens Thomson Mason, consisting primarily of Mason supporters, agreed in December 1836 to accept the U.P. in exchange for the Toledo Strip.

In January 1837, the U.S. Congress admitted Michigan as a state of the Union. At the time, Michigan was considered the losing party in the compromise. The land in the Upper Peninsula was described in a federal report as a "sterile region on the shores of Lake Superior destined by soil and climate to remain forever a wilderness."

This belief changed when rich mineral deposits (primarily copper and iron) were discovered in the 1840s. The Upper Peninsula's mines produced more mineral wealth than the California Gold Rush, especially after shipping was improved by the opening of the Soo Locks in 1855 and docks in Marquette in 1859. The Upper Peninsula supplied 90% of America's copper by the 1860s. It was the largest supplier of iron ore by the 1890s, and production continued to a peak in the 1920s, but sharply declined shortly afterward. The last copper mine closed in 1995, although the majority of mines had closed decades before. Some iron mining continues near Marquette.

The Upper Falls of the Tahquamenon River, near the northern shore of the peninsula.

Thousands of Americans and immigrants moved to the area during the mining boom, prompting the federal government to create Fort Wilkins near Copper Harbor to maintain order. The first wave were the Cornish from England, with centuries of mining experience; followed by Irish, Germans, and French Canadians. During the 1890s, Finnish immigrants began settling there in large numbers, forming the population plurality in the North-Western half of the peninsula. In the early 20th century, 75% of the population was foreign-born.

Geography

The Upper Peninsula contains 16,452 square miles (42,610 km²), almost one-third of the land area of the state (exclusive of territorial waters, which constitute about 40% of Michigan's total jurisdictional area). The maximum east-west distance in the Upper Peninsula is about 320 miles (515 km), and the maximum north-south distance is about 125 miles (200 km). It is bounded on the north by Lake Superior, on the east by St. Mary's River, on the south by Lake Michigan and Lake Huron, and on the west by Wisconsin and (counting the water border on Lake Superior) by Minnesota. It has about 1,700 miles (2,700 km) of continuous shoreline with the Great Lakes. There are about 4,300 inland lakes, the largest of which is Lake Gogebic, and 12,000 miles (19,000 km) of streams.

Pictured Rocks National Lakeshore

The peninsula is divided between the flat, swampy areas in the east, part of the Great Lakes Plain, and the steeper, more rugged western half, called the Superior Upland, part of the Canadian Shield. The rock in the western portion is the result of volcanic eruptions and is estimated to be at least 3.5 billion years old (much older than the eastern portion) and contains the region's ore resources. Banded-iron formations were deposited 2000 [1] million years ago; this is the Marquette Range Supergroup. A considerable amount of bedrock is visible. Mount Arvon, the highest point in Michigan, is found in the region, as well as the Porcupine and Huron Mountains. All of the higher areas are the remnants of ancient peaks, worn down over millions of years by erosion and glaciers.

The Keweenaw Peninsula is the northernmost part of the peninsula. It projects into Lake Superior and was the site of the first copper boom in the United States, part of a larger region of the peninsula called the Copper Country. Copper Island is its northernmost section.

About one third of the peninsula is government owned recreational forest land today, including the Ottawa National Forest and Hiawatha National Forest. Although heavily logged in the 19th century, the majority of the land was forested with mature trees by the 1970s.

Further information: Protected areas of Michigan

Wildlife

The Upper Peninsula contains a large variety of wildlife. Some of the mammals found in the U.P. include shrews, moles, mice, white tailed deer, moose, black bears, gray & red foxes, wolves, river otters, martens, fishers, cougars,bobcats, coyotes, snowshoe hares, cotton-tail rabbits, chipmunks, squirrels, raccoons and bats. There is a large variety of birds, including hawks, osprey, gulls, hummingbirds, chickadees, robins, woodpeckers, warblers, and bald eagles. In terms of reptiles and amphibians, the U.P. has common garter snakes, red bellied snakes, pine snakes, northern water snakes, brown snakes, eastern garter snakes, eastern fox snakes, eastern ribbon back snakes, smooth green snakes, northern ringneck snakes, Eastern Milk snakes (Mackinac and Marquette counties) and Eastern Hognose snakes (Menominee County only), plus snapping turtles, wood turtles, and painted turtles (the state reptile), green frogs, bull frogs, northern leopard frogs, and salamanders. Lakes and rivers contain many fish like walleye, Northern Pike, Trout, Salmon, and bass. The U.P. also contains many shellfish, such as clams, aquatic snails, and crayfish.

The American Bird Conservancy and the National Audubon Society have designated several locations as internationally Important Bird Areas.

There are also many invasive species that are primarily brought in the ballast water of foreign ships, usually from the ocean bordering Northeastern Asia. This water is dumped directly into the Great Lakes, depositing a variety of fresh and salt water fish and invertebrates. Most notably being the zebra muscle, Dreissena polymorpha. There are also many plant species that have been transported to the Great Lakes, including Purple Loosestrife Lythrum salicaria.

Climate

The Upper Peninsula has a humid continental climate (*Dfb* in the Köppen climate classification system). The Great Lakes have a great effect on most of the peninsula. Winters tend to be long, cold, and snowy for most of the peninsula, and because of its northern latitude, the daylight hours are short— around 8 hours between sunrise and sunset in the winter. Lake Superior has the greatest effect on the area, especially the northern and western parts. Many areas get in excess of 100–250 inches (250–630 cm) of snow per year—especially in the Keweenaw Peninsula and Baraga, Marquette and Alger counties, where Lake Superior contributes to lake-effect snow, making them a prominent part of the midwestern snow belt.

A cabin in the U.P. after a snowfall

Records of 390 inches (990 cm) of snow or more have been set in many communities in this area. The Keweenaw Peninsula averages more snowfall than almost anywhere in the United States—more than anywhere east of the Mississippi River and the most of all non-mountainous regions of the continental United States. Because of the howling storms across Lake Superior, which cause dramatic amounts of precipitation, it has been said that the lake-effect snow makes the Keweenaw Peninsula the snowiest place east of the Rockies. Herman, Michigan, averages 236 inches (600 cm) of snow every year. Lake-effect snow can cause blinding whiteouts in just minutes, and some storms can last days.

The area along the Wisconsin border has a more continental climate since most of its weather does not arrive from the lakes. Summers tend to be warmer and winter nights much colder. Coastal communities have temperatures tempered by the Great Lakes. In summer, it might be 10 °F (5 °C) cooler at lakeside than it is inland, and the opposite effect is seen in winter. The area of the Upper Peninsula north of Green Bay though Menominee and Escanaba (and extending west to Iron River) does not have the extreme weather and precipitation found to the north. Locally it is known as "the banana belt."

Time zones

Like the entire Lower Peninsula of Michigan, most of the Upper Peninsula observes Eastern Time. However, the four counties bordering Wisconsin are in the Central Time zone.

In 1967, when the Uniform Time Act came into effect, the Upper Peninsula went under year-round CST, with no daylight saving time. In 1973, the majority of the peninsula switched to Eastern Time; only the four western counties of Gogebic, Iron, Dickinson, and Menominee continue to observe Central Time.

Government

There are fifteen counties in the Upper Peninsula (see map).

State prisons are located in Baraga, Marquette, Munising, Newberry, Marenisco and Kincheloe.

Politics

The U.P. tends to vote for the Democratic Party, which is commonly considered to be politically liberal, however its people tend to be culturally conservative. The vote during the 2008 presidential election ended with some of the counties in the Upper Peninsula going for the Democratic Party, and others for the Republican Party. The breakdown of the 2008 presidential election by county was as follows:

Election results of the 2008 Presidential Election by County in the Upper Peninsula

County	Registered Voters	Votes Cast	McCain/Palin	Obama/Biden	Result
Alger	4,790	4,750	2,188	2,472	Dem
Baraga	3,699	3,644	1,846	1,725	Rep
Chippewa	16,869	16,708	8,267	8,184	Rep
Delta	19,231	19,064	8,763	9,974	Dem
Dickinson	13,463	13,311	7,049	5,995	Rep
Gogebic	8,366	8,264	3,330	4,757	Dem
Houghton	16,116	15,972	8,101	7,476	Rep
Iron	6,249	6,162	2,947	3,080	Dem
Keweenaw	1,428	1,410	756	610	Rep
Luce	2,769	2,740	1,490	1,191	Rep
Mackinac	6,466	6,396	3,268	3,027	Rep
Marquette	33,624	33,185	12,906	19,635	Dem
Menominee	11,166	11,072	4,855	5,981	Dem
Ontonagon	3,974	3,885	1,823	1,966	Dem
Schoolcraft	4,393	4,326	2,058	2,184	Dem
TOTAL	152,603	150,889	69,647	78,257	Dem

Bart Stupak (Dem) currently represents Michigan's 1st congressional district, which includes the Upper Peninsula. In 2006 incumbent Governor Jennifer Granholm (Dem) received a majority of the votes from the Upper Peninsula to help her win re-election to her second four-year term.

Superior (proposed state)

Main article: Superior (proposed state)

Superior is the name of a longstanding 51st state proposal for the secession of the Upper Peninsula from the rest of Michigan. Named for Lake Superior, the idea has gained serious attention at times. Because stronger connections to the rest of the state exist since completion of the Mackinac Bridge, the proposal's future is vague. Several prominent legislators, including local politician Dominic Jacobetti, attempted to gain passage of the bill in the 1970s, with little traction.

Demographics

The Upper Peninsula remains a predominantly rural region. As of the 2000 census, the region had a population of 317,258, which was predicted to have fallen to 308,319 according to the Census Bureau's July 1, 2008 estimate.

According to the 2000 census, only 91,624 people live in the twelve towns of at least 4,000 people, covering 96.5 square miles (155.365 km²). Only 114,544 people live in the 21 towns and villages of at least 2,000 people, which cover 123.7 square miles (320.4 km²)—less than 1% of the peninsula's land area.

Cities and Villages of the Upper Peninsula

City	Population	Area (sq mi)
Marquette	19,661	11.4
Sault Ste. Marie	16,542	14.8
Escanaba	13,140	12.7
Menominee	9,131	5.2
Iron Mountain	8,154	7.2
Houghton	7,134	4.3
Ishpeming	6,535	8.7
Ironwood	6,293	6.6
Kingsford	5,549	4.3
Gladstone	5,266	5.0
Negaunee	4,576	13.8
Hancock	4,323	2.5
Manistique	3,583	3.2

Iron River	3,122	3.5
Norway	2,959	8.8
Newberry	2,686	1.0
St. Ignace	2,678	2.7
Munising	2,539	5.4
Bessemer	2,148	5.5
Laurium	2,126	0.7
L'Anse	2,107	2.6
Wakefield	2,085	8.0
TOTAL	114,544	123.7

Upper Peninsula Land Area and Population Density by County

County	Population	Land Area (sq mi)	Population Density (per sq mi)
Alger	9,862	918	10.7
Baraga	8,735	904	9.7
Chippewa	38,413	1561	24.7
Delta	38,520	1170	32.9
Dickinson	27,427	766	35.8
Gogebic	17,370	1102	15.8
Houghton	36,016	1012	35.6
Iron	13,138	1166	11.3
Keweenaw	2,301	541	4.3
Luce	7,024	903	7.8
Mackinac	11,943	1022	11.7
Marquette	64,634	1821	35.5
Menominee	25,109	1043	24.3
Ontonagon	7,818	1312	6.0
Schoolcraft	8,903	1178	7.6
TOTAL	317,258	16,420	19.3

The Upper Peninsula is one of the few regions in the United States that experiences population decline. Although not every county in the Upper Peninsula has a declining population, this phenomenon does have a significant impact on the social and economic aspects of many of its communities and citizens. Some of the contributing factors to the Upper Peninsula's shifts in population are the boom and bust cycles of the timber and mining industries, as well as the severity of its winters.[citation needed] Some areas in the Upper Peninsula are more prone to declining population than others, with the six westernmost counties being the most dramatic, going from a 1920 level of 153,674 people (representing 59% of the total population of the entire Upper Peninsula) to a 2000 census level of 85,378 persons (dropping to 29% of the total Upper Peninsula's population). It is quite common to see abandoned buildings and ruins in this area; there are even a number of ghost towns that are slowly succumbing to the ubiquitous forest.[citation needed]

Typical ruins found in the western U.P.

Generally speaking, the population of the Upper Peninsula grew throughout the 19th Century, and then leveled off and even experienced decline during the 20th Century, as can readily be seen in the tables below. The data for these tables is from the U.S. Census; A "↑" indicates an increase in population from the previous census, and a "↓" indicates a decrease in population from the previous census.

19th Century Population by Census Year of the Upper Peninsula by County

County	1830	1840	1850	1860	1870	1880	1890	1900
Alger	N/A	N/A	N/A	N/A	N/A	N/A	1,238↑	5,868↑
Baraga	N/A	N/A	N/A	N/A	N/A	1,804↑	3,036↑	4,320↑
Chippewa	626↑	534↓	898↑	1,603↑	1,689↑	5,248↑	12,018↑	21,338↑
Delta	N/A	N/A	N/A	1,172↑	2,542↑	6,812↑	15,330↑	23,881↑
Dickinson	N/A	N/A	N/A	N/A	N/A	N/A	N/A	17,890↑
Gogebic	N/A	N/A	N/A	N/A	N/A	N/A	13,166↑	16,738↑
Houghton	N/A	N/A	708↑	9,234↑	13,879↑	22,473↑	35,389↑	66,063↑
Iron	N/A	N/A	N/A	N/A	N/A	N/A	4,432↑	8,990↑
Keweenaw	N/A	N/A	N/A	N/A	4,205↑	4,270↑	2,894↓	3,217↑

County								
Luce	N/A	N/A	N/A	N/A	N/A	N/A	2,455↑	2,983↑
Mackinac	877↑	923↑	3,598↑	1,938↓	1,716↓	2,902↑	7,830↑	7,703↓
Marquette	N/A	N/A	136↑	2,821↑	15,033↑	25,394↑	39,521↑	41,239↑
Menominee	N/A	N/A	N/A	N/A	1,791↑	11,987↑	33,639↑	27,046↓
Ontonagon	N/A	N/A	389↑	4,568↑	2,845↓	2,565↓	3,756↑	6,197↑
Schoolcraft	N/A	N/A	16↑	78↑	N/A	1,575↑	5,818↑	7,889↑
TOTAL	1,503↑	1,457↓	5,037↑	12,180↑	29,821↑	62,557↑	145,133↑	95,299↑

20th & 21st Centuries Population by Census Year of the Upper Peninsula by County

County	1910	1920	1930	1940	1950	1960	1970	1980	1990	2000	2010
Alger	7,675↑	9,983↑	9,327↓	10,167↑	10,007↓	9,250↓	8,568↓	9,225↑	8,972↓	9,862↑	N/A
Baraga	6,125↑	7,662↑	9,168↑	9,356↑	8,037↓	7,151↓	7,789↑	8,484↑	7,954↓	8,735↑	N/A
Chippewa	24,472↑	24,818↑	25,047↑	27,807↑	29,206↑	32,655↑	32,412↓	29,029↓	34,604↑	38,413↑	N/A
Delta	30,108↑	30,909↑	32,280↑	34,037↑	32,913↓	34,298↑	35,924↑	38,947↑	37,780↓	38,520↑	N/A
Dickinson	20,524↑	19,456↓	29,941↑	28,731↓	24,844↓	23,917↓	23,753↓	25,341↑	26,831↑	27,427↑	N/A
Gogebic	23,333↑	33,225↑	31,577↓	31,797↑	27,053↓	24,370↓	20,676↓	19,686↓	18,052↓	17,370↓	N/A
Houghton	88,098↑	71,930↓	52,851↓	47,631↓	39,771↓	34,654↓	34,652↓	37,872↑	35,446↓	36,016↑	N/A
Iron	15,164↑	22,107↑	20,805↓	20,243↓	17,692↓	17,184↓	13,813↓	13,635↓	13,175↓	13,138↓	N/A
Keweenaw	7,156↑	6,322↓	5,076↓	4,004↓	2,918↓	2,417↓	2,264↓	1,963↓	1,701↓	2,301↑	N/A
Luce	4,004↑	6,149↑	6,528↑	7,423↑	8,147↑	7,827↓	6,789↓	6,659↓	5,763↓	7,024↑	N/A
Mackinac	9,249↑	8,026↓	8,783↑	9,438↑	9,287↓	10,853↑	9,660↓	10,178↑	10,674↑	11,943↑	N/A
Marquette	46,739↑	45,786↓	44,076↓	47,144↑	47,654↑	56,154↑	64,686↑	74,101↑	70,887↓	64,634↓	N/A
Menominee	25,648↓	23,778↓	23,652↓	24,883↑	25,299↑	24,685↓	24,587↓	26,201↑	24,920↓	25,109↑	N/A
Ontonagon	8,650↑	12,428↑	11,114↓	11,359↑	10,282↓	10,584↑	10,548↓	9,861↓	8,854↓	7,818↓	N/A
Schoolcraft	8,681↑	9,977↑	8,451↓	9,524↑	9,148↓	8,953↓	8,226↓	8,575↑	8,302↓	8,903↑	N/A

| TOTAL | 237,528↑ | 260,626↑ | 265,825↑ | 275,913↑ | 262,487↓ | 304,952↑ | 304,347↓ | 319,757↑ | 313,915↓ | 317,213↑ | N/A |

Economy

Industries

The Upper Peninsula is rich in mineral deposits including iron, copper, nickel and silver. Small amounts of gold have also been discovered and mined. In the 19th century, mining dominated the economy, and the U.P. became home to many isolated company towns. For many years, mines in the Keweenaw Peninsula were the world's largest producers of copper. The mines began declining as early as 1913, with most closing temporarily during the Great Depression. Mines reopened during World War II, but almost all quickly closed after the war ended. The last copper mine in the Copper Country was the White Pine Mine, which closed in 1995.

Ever since logging of white pine began in the 1880s, timber has been an important industry. However, the stands of hemlock and hardwood went under-exploited until the mid-twentieth century as selection cutting was practiced in the western reaches of the forest. Because of the highly seasonal climate and the short growing season, agriculture is limited in the Upper Peninsula, though potatoes, strawberries and a few other small fruits are grown.

Tourism has become the main industry in recent decades. In 2005, ShermanTravel, LLC listed the Upper Peninsula as No. 10 in its assessment of all travel destinations worldwide. The article was republished in April 2006 by MSN.com. The peninsula has extensive coastline on the Great Lakes, large tracts of state and national forests, cedar swamps, more than 150 waterfalls, and low population densities. Because of the camping, boating, fishing, snowmobiling, hunting, and hiking opportunities, many Lower Peninsula and Wisconsin families spend their vacations in the U.P. Tourists also go there from Detroit, Chicago, Milwaukee and other metropolitan areas.

Notable attractions

- Au Train Falls
- Bond Falls
- Calumet Theatre
- Calumet Downtown Historic District
- Copper Harbor
- Copper Peak, Ironwood Township – Largest man made ski flying complex in the western hemisphere
- DeYoung Family Zoo
- Fayette Historic State Park
- Fort Mackinac

- Garlyn Zoo
- Grand Hotel (Mackinac Island)
- Grand Island National Recreation Area
- The Great Lakes Shipwreck Museum
- Iron County Historical Museum Complex – Caspian
- Iron Industry Museum – Negaunee
- Iron Mountain Iron Mine – Vulcan
- Isle Royale National Park
- Keweenaw National Historical Park
- Keweenaw Waterway and Portage Lake Lift Bridge
- Kitch-iti-kipi
- Lake Superior
- Lake Superior State University, Lakers
- Laughing Whitefish Falls
- The Mackinac Bridge
- Mackinac Island
- Marquette Arts and Culture Center – Marquette
- The Marquette Lighthouse
- Marquette Mountain Ski Resort
- Michigan Technological University, Huskies
- Mount Bohemia ski center (with the highest vertical drop – 900 feet (270 m) – in the Midwest)
- Munising Falls
- National Ski Hall of Fame
- Northern Michigan University, Wildcats
- Marquette Ore Dock
- Paulding Light
- Pictured Rocks National Lakeshore
- Pine Mountain ski jump in Iron Mountain is one of the largest artificial ski jumps in the world.
- Porcupine Mountains State Park
- Quincy Copper Mine offering guided tours.
- Seney National Wildlife Refuge
- Ski Brule in Iron River.
- The Soo Locks
- Suicide Hill Ski Jump, Ishpeming, Michigan
- Sylvania Wilderness
- Tahquamenon Falls State Park
- Upper Peninsula Children's Museum [2] – Marquette

Casinos

American Indian casinos contribute to the tourist attractions and are popular in the U.P. Originally the casinos were simple, one-room affairs. Some of the casinos are now quite elaborate and are being developed as part of resort and conference facilities, including features such as golf courses, pool and spa, dining, and rooms to accommodate guests.

- Bay Mills Resort & Casino – Brimley
- Island Resort & Casino – Bark River
- Kewadin Casinos – Christmas; Hessel; Manistique; St. Ignace; Sault Ste. Marie
- Kings Club Casino – Brimley
- Lac Vieux Desert Casino – Watersmeet
- Ojibwa Casinos – Baraga; Marquette

Transportation

The Upper Peninsula is separated from the Lower by the Straits of Mackinac, five miles (8 km) across at the narrowest, and is connected to it by the Mackinac Bridge at St. Ignace, one of the longest suspension bridges in the world. Until the bridge was completed in 1957, travel between the two peninsulas was difficult and slow (and sometimes even impossible during winter months). In 1881, the Mackinac Transportation Company was established by three railroads, the Michigan Central Railroad, the Grand Rapids and Indiana Railroad, and the Detroit, Mackinac and Marquette Railroad, to operate a railroad car ferry across the Straits. Beginning in 1923, the State of Michigan operated automobile ferries between the two peninsulas. At the busiest times of year the wait was several hours long. In winter, travel was possible over the ice only after the straits had solidly frozen.

Straits of Mackinac and bridge in winter

Despite its rural character, there are public buses in several counties of the Upper Peninsula.

Automobiles

The primary means of transportation in the Upper Peninsula is by automobile. It is served by one interstate and several U.S. and Michigan state highways. Aside from the interstate, there are no speed limits above 55 mph.

Major highways

- I-75 crosses the eastern portion of the Upper Peninsula from the Straits of Mackinac on the south to Sault Ste. Marie and the border with Canada on the north. There it connects with Sault Ste. Marie International Bridge into Canada. and Sault Ste. Marie, Ontario.
- US 2 runs from St. Ignace west to Ironwood and into Wisconsin.
- US 41 enters at Menominee and goes north to Copper Harbor.
- US 45 runs from Ontonagon south into Wisconsin.
- US 141 runs from US 41 in Baraga County south to Wisconsin. Re-enters Michigan briefly at Iron Mountain & Kingsford and then exits south into Wisconsin.
- M-28 runs east–west across the U.P. from Wakefield to south of Sault Ste. Marie,

Great Lakes Circle Tour

The Great Lakes Circle Tour is a designated scenic road system connecting all of the Great Lakes and the St. Lawrence River.

Airports

Main article: Airports Of The Upper Peninsula Of Michigan

There are 43 airports in the Upper Peninsula.

There are six airports with commercial passenger service: Gogebic-Iron County Airport north of Ironwood, Houghton County Memorial Airport southwest of Calumet, Ford Airport west of Iron Mountain, Sawyer International Airport south of Marquette, Delta County Airport in Escanaba, and Chippewa County International Airport south of Sault Ste. Marie.

There are 19 other public use airports with a hard surface runway. These are used for general aviation and charter. Notably, Mackinac Island, Beaver Island, and Drummond Island are all accessible by airports.

There are 5 public access airports with turf runways.

There are 13 airports for the private use of their owners.

There is only one control tower in the Upper Peninsula, at Sawyer.

Ferries and bridges

The Eastern Upper Peninsula Transportation Authority operates car ferries in its area. These include ferries for Sugar Island, Neebish Island, and Drummond Island. Three ferry companies run passenger ferries from St. Ignace to Mackinac Island.

The three major bridges in the Upper Peninsula are:

- Mackinac Bridge, connecting Northern Michigan to the Upper Peninsula;
- Sault Ste. Marie International Bridge, which connects the city of Sault Ste. Marie to its twin city of Sault Ste. Marie in Canada; and
- Portage Lift Bridge, which crosses Portage Lake. The Portage Lift Bridge is the world's heaviest and widest double-decked vertical lift bridge. Its center span "lifts" to provide 100 feet (30 m) of clearance for ships. Since rail traffic was discontinued in the Keweenaw, the lower deck is used to accommodate snowmobile traffic in the winter. As the only land-based link between the north and south sections of the Keweenaw Peninsula, the bridge is crucial to transportation.

Railways

- Lake Superior and Ishpeming Railroad: Transports iron ore over a 16-mile (26-km) line from the Empire-Tilden Mine (operated by Cleveland-Cliffs), south of Ishpeming, to Marquette's port on Lake Superior.
- Two railroads originally crossed the Upper Peninsula east to west: the Minneapolis, St. Paul and Sault Ste. Marie Railway, informally known as the Soo Line, running west from Sault Ste. Marie roughly along the Lake Michigan shore, and the Duluth, South Shore and Atlantic Railroad running west from St. Ignace roughly along the Lake Superior shore. In 1960, both railroads were merged into the Soo Line Railroad, the U.S. arm of the Canadian Pacific Railway. The Soo Line trackage in the Upper Peninsula was purchased by the Wisconsin Central Railroad in 1987. In 1997, the Wisconsin Central also purchased from the Union Pacific Railroad the former Chicago and North Western Railway line running into the Upper Peninsula from Wisconsin. The Wisconsin Central was in turn purchased by the Canadian National Railway in 2001. The Canadian National now operates much of the remaining railroad trackage in the Upper Peninsula.
- Escanaba and Lake Superior Railroad: Chartered in 1898, the E&LS is an industrial beltline railroad with 347 miles (558 km) of trackage connecting Escanaba, Ontonagon, Republic, and Green Bay, Wisconsin, with a common junction at Channing, and a spur to Nestoria from Sidnaw.

Education

The Upper Peninsula of Michigan has three state universities (Lake Superior State University in Sault Ste. Marie, Michigan Technological University in Houghton, and Northern Michigan University in Marquette), one private university (Finlandia University located in Hancock, Michigan, on the Keweenaw Peninsula), and three community colleges (Bay Mills Community College in Brimley, Bay de Noc Community College in Escanaba and Gogebic Community College in Ironwood).

Culture

Early settlers included multiple waves of people from Nordic countries. There are still Swedish- and Finnish-speaking communities in many areas of the Upper Peninsula today. People of Finnish ancestry make up 16% of the peninsula's population. The U.P. is home to the highest concentration of Finns outside Europe and the only counties of the United States where a plurality of residents claim Finnish ancestry. The Finnish sauna and the concept of sisu have been adopted widely by residents of the Upper Peninsula. The television program *Finland Calling*, filmed at Marquette station WLUC-TV, is the only Finnish-language television broadcast in the United States; it has aired since March 25, 1962. Finlandia University, America's only college with Finnish roots, is located in Hancock. Street signs in Hancock appear in English and Finnish to celebrate this heritage.

"Da Yoopers Tourist Trap" near Ishpeming, features a host of gaudy items in its museum and store that play up Yooper stereotypes

Other sizeable ethnic communities in the Upper Peninsula include French-Canadian, German, Cornish, Italian, and American Indian ancestry.

Upper Peninsula natives speak a dialect influenced by Scandinavian and French-Canadian speech. A popular bumper sticker, a parody of the "Say YES to Michigan" slogan promoted by state tourism officials, shows an outline of the Upper Peninsula and the slogan, "Say yah to da U.P., eh!" The dialect and culture are captured in many songs by Da Yoopers, a comedy music and skit troupe from Ishpeming, Michigan.

The Mining Journal, based in Marquette, is the only daily newspaper that publishes on Sundays. The Sunday edition is distributed across the entire U.P., while on the other six days of the way it publishes in its local area only. There are other newspapers, such as *The Daily News* of Iron Mountain, The Menominee County Journal [3], of Stephenson, *The Daily Mining Gazette* of Houghton, The Daily Press of Escanaba, and the *Sault Ste. Marie Evening News* that serve the rest of the U.P.

The Keweenaw peninsula is home to several ski areas. Mont Ripley, just outside of Houghton, is popular among students of Michigan Technological University (the university actually owns the mountain). Further up the peninsula in the small town of Lac La Belle is Mt. Bohemia. A skiing purist's resort, Bohemia is a self proclaimed "experts only" mountain, and it does not groom its heavily gladed slopes. Another ski area is Pine Mountain located in Iron Mountain.

Regional identity

Today, the Upper Peninsula is home to 328,000 people—only about 3% of the state's population—living in almost one-third of the state's land area. Residents are known as Yoopers, (from "U.P.ers") and many consider themselves Yoopers before they consider themselves Michiganders. (People living in the Lower Peninsula are commonly called "trolls" by Upper Peninsula residents, as they live "Under da Bridge".) This regionalism is not only a result of the physical separation of the two peninsulas, but also the history of the state.

Residents of the western Upper Peninsula take on some of the cultural identities of both Wisconsin and Michigan. In terms of sports fandom, residents often gravitate toward the nearby Wisconsin teams, particularly the Green Bay Packers. This is a result of both proximity and the broadcast and print media of the area. The four counties that border Wisconsin are also in the Central Time Zone, unlike the rest of Michigan, which is on Eastern time.

A Yooper pasty (beef)

A trip downstate is often rather difficult: a trip from Ironwood to Detroit is roughly 600 miles (960 km) long, more than twice the distance to Minneapolis and almost as long as a trip to St. Louis. Such a trip is made more difficult by the lack of freeways: a short section of I-75 is the only interstate in the U.P. Commonly, people of the western U.P. will go to Minneapolis or Wisconsin for trips. Residents of the northeastern part of the U.P. may cross the Sault Ste. Marie International Bridge to Canada more often than they cross the Mackinac Bridge to the Lower Peninsula, and they often associate more closely with Northern Ontario.

Cuisine

The Upper Peninsula has a distinctive local cuisine. The pasty (pronounced pass tee), a kind of meat turnover originally brought to the region by Cornish miners, is popular among locals and tourists alike. Pasty varieties include chicken, venison, pork, hamburger, and pizza. Many restaurants serve potato sausage and *cudighi*, a spicy Italian meat.

Finnish immigrants contributed *nisu*, a cardamom-flavored sweet bread; *pannukakku*, a variant on the pancake with a custard flavor; *viili* (sometimes spelled "fellia"), a stretchy, fermented Finnish milk; and *korppu*, hard slices of toasted cinnamon bread, traditionally dipped in coffee. Some Finnish foods such as *juustoa* [4] (squeeky cheese) and *sauna makkara* (a ring-bologna sausage) have become so ubiquitous in Upper Peninsula cuisine that they are now commonly-found in most grocery stores and supermarkets.

Maple syrup is a highly prized local delicacy. Fresh Great Lakes fish, such as the lake trout, whitefish, and (in the spring) smelt are widely eaten, despite concerns about PCB contamination and elevated mercury concentrations. Smoked fish is also popular. Thimbleberry and Chokecherry jam is a treat.

Notable residents

- Former University of Michigan football coach Lloyd Carr is an alumnus of Northern Michigan University; he was quarterback for the school's football team during an undefeated season in 1967. He graduated from NMU in 1968 with his B.S. in education and went on to earn his M.A. in education administration at NMU in 1970.
- James Tolkan, an American actor often cast as a strict, overbearing, bald-headed authority who played roles in *Back to the Future* and *Top Gun* was born in Calumet, Michigan.
- Robert J. Flaherty, a filmmaker who directed and produced the first commercially successful feature length documentary film Nanook of the North in 1922 is from Iron Mountain.
- George Gipp, the "Gipper"—immortalized in the film *Knute Rockne, All American* by Ronald Reagan—was born in Laurium. He was the first All-American at the Notre Dame football program.
- Clarence L. "Kelly" Johnson, aircraft engineer and aeronautical innovator, was born in Ishpeming.
- John Lautner, a native of Marquette and alumnus of Northern Michigan University, was one of Frank Lloyd Wright's most successful Taliesin fellows. His Modernist residence, Chemosphere, is a Los Angeles landmark.
- Former San Francisco 49ers and Detroit Lions head coach Steve Mariucci and Michigan State basketball coach Tom Izzo are both natives of Iron Mountain. Both went to Northern Michigan University, where Mariucci was quarterback of the Wildcats' 1975 NCAA Division II national championship team.
- Terry O'Quinn, actor, was born in Sault Sainte Marie in 1952. O'Quinn most recently appeared with a recurring role as John Locke in the popular TV show, *Lost*.
- Chase Osborn was the only Governor of Michigan from the Upper Peninsula (1911–1913).
- Pam Reed is an ultrarunner who currently resides in Tucson, Arizona. She grew up in Palmer, Michigan, and graduated from Michigan Technological University.
- Mike Shaw, professional wrestler, was born in Skandia. He wrestled in the WWF as Bastion Booger and in the WCW as Norman the Lunatic.
- Howard Schultz, chairman of Starbucks Coffee Co., is a Northern Michigan University alumnus.

- Glenn T. Seaborg, a chemist and major contributor in the discovery of several of the transuranium elements, was born in Ishpeming. Before his death in 1999, he was the only living person to have a chemical element named after him (seaborgium, abbreviated as Sg and with atomic number 106). This name caused controversy because Seaborg was still alive, but eventually it was accepted by international chemists. Though he lived most of his life in California, the Seaborg Center at Northern Michigan University is named in his honor.
- Matthew Songer, founder and CEO of Pioneer Surgical Technology, lives in Marquette.
- Mary Chase Perry Stratton founder of Pewabic Pottery, was born in Hancock, Michigan.
- Art Van Damme, jazz accordionist, was born in Norway, Michigan.
- Hon. John D. Voelker, Justice of the Michigan Supreme Court, wrote the best selling book *Anatomy of a Murder* under the pen name Robert Traver. The movie — filmed in Big Bay and Ishpeming (with some courtroom scenes in Marquette) — was directed by Otto Preminger.
- Steven Wiig, actor in the film *Into the Wild* and musician, was born and raised in Negaunee, Michigan, attended Northern Michigan University and works with the band Metallica.

See also

- List of counties in Michigan
- List of Michigan county name etymologies

Further reading

- Burt, Williams A.; Hubbard, Bela (1846). *Reports on the Mineral Region of Lake Superior* [5]. Buffalo: L. Danforth. ISBN 0665510098. 113 pages.
- Lankton, Larry (2010). *Hollowed Ground: Copper Mining and Community Building on Lake Superior, 1840s–1990s*. Detroit: Wayne State University Press. 376 pages. Focuses on three companies, Calumet & Hecla, Copper Range, and Quincy, in a study of native copper mining and copper-sulfide mining on Upper Michigan's Keweenaw Peninsula.

External links

- Clarke Historical Library, Central Michigan University, Bibliography on Michigan [6], arranged by counties and regions
- Beacons in the Night: Michigan Lighthouse Chronology [13] Clarke Historical Library
- Michigan Geology [6], Clarke Historical Library
- Great Lakes Coast Watch [7]
- Michigan Department of Natural Resources website [8], harbors, hunting, resources and more
- Michigan Historic Markers [9]

- Michigan's Official Economic Development and Travel Site [10], including interactive map, information on attractions, museums, etc.
- Map of Upper Peninsula Counties and Minor Civil Divisions [11]
- Michigan's Official Economic Development and Travel Site [10]
- Finland Calling [12] the WLUC TV-6 weekly Sunday morning show that has aired since 1962, hosted since then by Karl Pellonpaa.

Geographical coordinates: 46°14'00"N 86°21'00"W

Lake Superior

Lake Superior	

Landsat image	
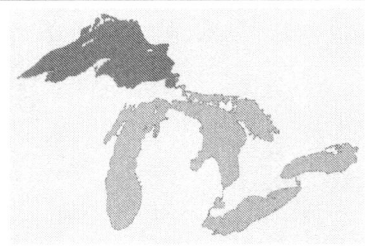	
Lake Superior and the other Great Lakes	
Location	North America
Group	Great Lakes
Coordinates	47°42′N 87°30′W
Lake type	Glacial
Primary inflows	Nipigon, St. Louis, Pigeon, Pic, White, Michipicoten, Kaministiquia Rivers
Primary outflows	St. Marys River
Catchment area	49305 sq mi (127700 km^2)
Basin countries	Canada, United States
Max. length	350 mi (560 km)
Max. width	160 mi (260 km)
Surface area	31820 sq mi (82400 km^2) Canadian portion 11081 sq mi (28700 km^2)
Average depth	482 ft (147 m)
Max. depth	1332 ft (406 m)
Water volume	2900 cu mi (12000 km^3)
Residence time	191 years

Shore length[1]	2725 mi (4385 km)
Surface elevation	600 ft (180 m)
Islands	Isle Royale, Apostle Islands, Slate Islands
Settlements	Thunder Bay, Ontario Duluth, Minnesota Sault Ste. Marie, Ontario Marquette, Michigan Superior, Wisconsin Sault Ste. Marie, Michigan
[1] Shore length is not a well-defined measure.	

Lake Superior (French: *Lac Supérieur*) is the largest of the five Great Lakes of North America. It is bounded to the north by the Canadian province of Ontario and the U.S. state of Minnesota, and to the south by the U.S. states of Wisconsin and Michigan. It is the largest freshwater lake in the world by surface area (but only if Lake Michigan and Lake Huron aren't considered one lake) and is the world's third-largest freshwater lake by volume.

Name

The Ojibwe call the lake *Gichigami*, meaning "big water." Henry Wadsworth Longfellow wrote the name as "Gitche Gumee" in The Song of Hiawatha. "The first French explorers approaching the great inland sea by way of the Ottawa River and Lake Huron during the 17th century referred to their discovery as *le lac superieur*. Properly translated, the expression means "Upper Lake," that is, the lake above Lake Huron. The lake was also called *Lac Tracy* by 17th century Jesuit missionaries." The English, upon taking control of the region from the French in the 1760's, following the French and Indian War, anglicized the lake's name to *Superior*, "on account of its being superior in magnitude to any of the lakes on that vast continent."

Hydrography

Lake Superior is the largest freshwater lake in the world by surface area, and empties into Lake Huron via the St. Marys River and the Soo Locks. Lake Baikal in Russia is larger by volume, as is Lake Tanganyika. The Caspian Sea, while larger than Lake Superior in both surface area and volume, is brackish; though presently isolated, historically the Caspian has been repeatedly connected to and isolated from the Mediterranean via the Black Sea.

Lake Superior has a surface area of 31820 square miles (82413 km^2), which is approximately the size of South Carolina. It has a maximum length of 350 miles (563 km) and maximum breadth of 160 miles (257 km). Its average depth is 482 feet (147 m) with a maximum depth of 1332 feet (406 m). Lake

Superior contains 2,900 cubic miles (12,100 km³) of water. There is enough water in Lake Superior to cover the entire land mass of North and South America with 1 foot (30 cm) of water. The shoreline of the lake stretches 2726 miles (4387 km) (including islands).

American limnologist J. Val Klump was the first person to reach the lowest depth of Lake Superior on July 30, 1985, as part of a scientific expedition, which, at 733 feet (223 m) below sea level, is the lowest spot on the continental interior of the United States and the second-lowest spot on the interior of the North American continent after the much deeper Great Slave Lake in Canada (458 metres (1503 ft) below sea level). (Though Crater Lake, not Lake Superior, is the deepest lake in the United States, Crater Lake's surface elevation is much higher and its deepest point is 4229 feet (1289 m) *above* sea level.)

The average temperature of the lake during the summer is about 40 degrees Fahrenheit (4.4 °C). Lake Superior is the largest, deepest and coldest of the Great Lakes. Superior could contain the volume of all the other Great Lakes and three more Lake Eries. Because of its size Superior has a retention time of 191 years.

Annual storms on Lake Superior regularly record wave heights of over 20 feet (6 m). Waves well over 30 feet (9 m) have been recorded.

Tributaries and outlet

The lake is fed by over 200 rivers. The largest include the Nipigon River, the St. Louis River, the Pigeon River, the Pic River, the White River, the Michipicoten River, the Bois Brule River and the Kaministiquia River. Lake Superior drains into Lake Huron by the St. Marys River. The rapids on the river necessitate the Sault Locks (pronounced "soo"), a part of the Great Lakes Waterway, to move boats over the 25 feet (8 m) height difference from Lake Huron.

Water levels

The lake's average surface elevation is 600 feet (183 m) above sea level. Until approximately 1887 the natural hydraulic conveyance through the St. Marys River rapids determined outflow from Lake Superior. By 1921 development in support of transportation and hydropower resulted in gates, locks, power canals and other control structures completely spanning St. Marys rapids. The regulating structure is known as the Compensating Works and is operated according to a regulation plan known as Plan 1977-A. The current water levels, including diversions of water from the Hudson Bay watershed, are governed by the International Lake Superior Board of Control which was established in 1914 by the International Joint Commission.

Lake Superior in winter, as seen from Duluth, Minnesota in December 2004.

Superior's water levels temporarily reached a new low in September 2007, slightly less than the previous record low in 1926. However, the water levels returned within a few days.

Historic High Water The lake fluctuates from month to month with the highest lake levels in October and November. The normal highwater mark is 1.17 feet (0.36 m) above datum (*601.1 ft or 183.2 metres*). In the summer of 1985, Lake Superior reached its highest level at 2.33 feet (0.71 m) above datum. The winter of 1986 set new highwater records through the winter and spring months

Ice on Lake Superior as seen from space (MODIS, March 3, 2009).

(January - June), ranging from 1.33 feet (0.41 m) to 1.833 feet (0.559 m) above Chart Datum.

Historic Low Water The lake fluctuates from month to month with the lowest lake levels in April and March. The normal lowwater mark is 0.33 feet (0.10 m) below datum (*601.1 ft or 183.2 metres*). In the winter of 1926 Lake Superior reached its lowest level at 1.58 feet (0.48 m) below datum. Additionally, the entire first half of the year (January - June) saw record low months. The low water was a continuation of the dropping lake levels from the previous year, 1925; which set lowwater records for October through December. During this nine-month period (Oct 1925-June 1926) water levels ranged from 1.58 feet (0.48 m) to 0.33 feet (0.10 m) below Chart Datum. In the summer of 2007 monthly historic lows were set; August at 0.66 feet (0.20 m), September at 0.58 feet (0.18 m).

Climate change

According to a study by professors at the University of Minnesota Duluth, Lake Superior may have warmed faster than its surrounding climate. Summer surface temperatures in the lake appeared to have increased about 4.5 Fahrenheit degrees (2.5 Celsius degrees) since 1979, compared with an approximately 2.7 Fahrenheit degree (1.5 Celsius degree) increase in the surrounding average air temperature. The increase in the lake's surface temperature may be related to the decreasing ice cover. Less winter ice cover allows more solar radiation to penetrate the lake and warm the water. If trends continue Lake Superior, which freezes over completely once every 20 years, could routinely be ice-free by 2040. These warmer temperatures can actually lead to more snow in the lake effect snow belts along the shores of the lake, especially in the Upper Peninsula of Michigan.

Geography

The largest island in Lake Superior is Isle Royale in the state of Michigan. Isle Royale contains several lakes, some of which also contain islands. Other large famous islands include Madeline Island in the state of Wisconsin and Michipicoten Island in the province of Ontario.

The larger cities on Lake Superior include: the twin ports of Duluth, Minnesota, and Superior, Wisconsin; Thunder Bay, Ontario; Marquette, Michigan; and the twin cities of Sault Ste. Marie, Michigan, and Sault Ste. Marie, Ontario. Duluth, at the western tip of Lake Superior, is the most inland point on the St. Lawrence Seaway and the most inland port in the world.

Among the scenic places on the lake are: the Apostle Islands National Lakeshore, Isle Royale National Park, Porcupine Mountains Wilderness State Park, Pukaskwa National Park, Lake Superior Provincial Park, Grand Island National Recreation Area, Sleeping Giant (Ontario) and Pictured Rocks National Lakeshore.

Great Lakes Circle Tour

The Great Lakes Circle Tour is a designated scenic road system connecting all of the Great Lakes and the St. Lawrence River.

Climate

Lake Superior's size creates a localized oceanic or maritime climate (more typically seen in locations like Nova Scotia). The water surface's slow reaction to temperature changes, seasonally ranging between 32°-55°F (0°-13°C) around 1970, helps to moderate surrounding air temperatures in the summer and winter, and creates lake effect snow in colder months. The hills and mountains that border the lake hold moisture and fog, particularly in the fall.

The lake's surface temperature has risen by 4.5 Fahrenheit degrees (2.5 Celsius degrees) since 1979.

Geology

The rocks of Lake Superior's North Shore date back to the early history of the earth. During the Precambrian (between 4.5-billion and 540-million years ago) magma forcing its way to the surface created the intrusive granites of the Canadian Shield. These ancient granites can be seen on the North Shore today. It was during the Penokean orogeny, part of the process that created the Great Lakes Tectonic Zone, that many valuable metals were deposited. The region surrounding the lake has proved to be rich in minerals. Copper, iron, silver, gold and nickel are or were the most frequently mined. Examples include the Hemlo gold mine near Marathon, copper at

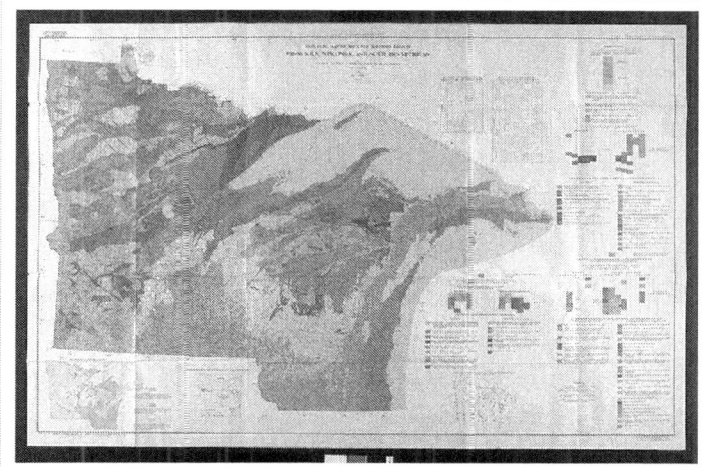

Bedrock geologic map of the U.S. area bordering Lake Superior: Minnesota, Wisconsin, and the Upper Peninsula of Michigan.

Point Mamainse, silver at Silver Islet and uranium at Theano Point.

The mountains steadily eroded, depositing layers of sediments which compacted and became limestone, dolostone, taconite and the shale at Kakabeka Falls.

The continent was later riven, creating one of the deepest rifts in the world. The lake lies in this long-extinct Mesoproterozoic rift valley, the Midcontinent Rift. Magma was injected between layers of sedimentary rock, forming diabase sills. This hard diabase protects the layers of sedimentary rock below, forming the flat-topped mesas in the Thunder Bay area.

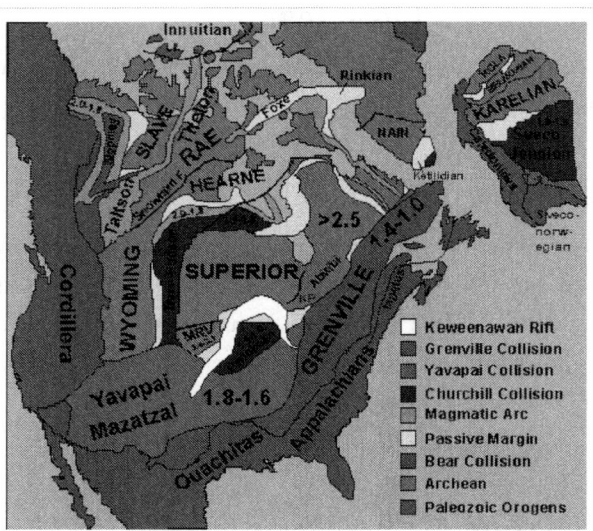

North American cratons and basement rock, showing the formation of the Midcontinent Rift containing today's Lake Superior.

Amethyst formed in some of the cavities created by the Midcontinent Rift and there are several amethyst mines in the Thunder Bay area.

Lava erupted from the rift and formed the black basalt rock of Michipicoten Island, Black Bay Peninsula, and St. Ignace Island.

During the Wisconsin glaciation 10,000 years ago, ice covered the region at a thickness of 1.25 miles (2.01 km). The land contours familiar today were carved by the advance and retreat of the ice sheet. The retreat left gravel, sand, clay and boulder deposits. Glacial meltwaters gathered in the Superior basin creating Lake Minong, a precursor to Lake Superior. Without the immense weight of the ice, the land rebounded, and a drainage outlet formed at Sault Ste. Marie, which would become known as St. Mary's River.

History

Pictographs at Lake Superior Provincial Park, Ontario

The first people came to the Lake Superior region 10,000 years ago after the retreat of the glaciers in the last Ice Age. They are known as the Plano, and they used stone-tipped spears to hunt caribou on the northwestern side of Lake Minong.

The next documented people were known as the Shield Archaic (c. 5000-500 BC). Evidence of this culture can be found at the eastern and western ends of the Canadian shore. They used bows and arrows, dugout canoes, fished, hunted, mined copper for tools and weapons, and established trading networks. They are believed to be the direct ancestors of the Ojibwe and Cree.

The Laurel people (c. 500 BC to AD 500) developed seine net fishing, evidence being found at rivers around Superior such as the Pic and Michipicoten.

Another culture known as the Terminal Woodland Indians (c. AD 900-1650) has been found. They were Algonkian people who hunted, fished and gathered berries. They used snow shoes, birch bark canoes and conical or domed lodges. At the mouth of the Michipicoten River, nine layers of encampments have been discovered. Most of the Pukaskwa Pits were likely made during this time.

The Anishinaabe, also known as the Ojibwe or Chippewa, have inhabited the Lake Superior region for over five hundred years and were preceded by the Dakota, Fox, Menominee, Nipigon, Noquet and Gros Ventres. They called Lake Superior *Anishnaabe Gichgamiing*, or "the Ojibwe's Ocean". After the arrival of Europeans, the Anishinaabe made themselves the middle-men between the French fur traders and other Native peoples. They soon became the dominant Indian nation in the region: they forced out the Sioux and Fox and won a victory against the Iroquois west of Sault Ste. Marie in 1662. By the mid-18th century, the Ojibwe occupied all of Lake Superior's shores.

In the 18th century, the fur trade in the region was booming, with the Hudson's Bay Company having a virtual monopoly. In 1783, however, the North West Company was formed to rival Hudson's Bay Company. The North West Company built forts on Lake Superior at Grand Portage, Nipigon, the Pic River, the Michipicoten River, and Sault Ste. Marie.

Reconstructed Great Hall, Grand Portage National Monument, Minnesota

But by 1821, with competition taking too great a toll on both, the companies merged under the Hudson's Bay Company name.

Many towns around the lake are either current or former mining areas, or engaged in processing or shipping. Today, tourism is another significant industry; the sparsely-populated Lake Superior country, with its rugged shorelines and wilderness, attracts tourists and adventurers.

Shipping

Lake Superior has been an important link in the Great Lakes Waterway, providing a route for the transportation of iron ore and other mined and manufactured materials. Large cargo vessels called lake freighters, as well as smaller ocean-going freighters, transport these commodities across Lake Superior.

Shipwrecks

See also: Great Storms of the North American Great Lakes

See also: List of shipwrecks of Isle Royale

According to shipwreck historian Frederick Stonehouse, the southern shore of Lake Superior between Grand Marais, Michigan, and Whitefish Point is known as the "Graveyard of the Great Lakes" and more ships have been lost around the Whitefish Point area than any other part of Lake Superior. These shipwrecks are now protected by the Whitefish Point Underwater Preserve. The SS *Edmund Fitzgerald* was the last major shipwreck on Lake Superior, sinking 17 miles (27 km) from Whitefish Point on November 10, 1975.

According to legend, "Lake Superior seldom gives up her dead". This is because of the unusually low temperature of the water, estimated at under 36 °F (2 °C) on average around 1970. Normally bacteria feeding on a sunken decaying body will generate gas inside the body, causing it to float to the surface after a few days. The water in Lake Superior is cold enough year-round to inhibit bacterial growth, and bodies tend to sink and never surface. This is alluded to in Gordon Lightfoot's ballad, "The Wreck of the *Edmund Fitzgerald*". The *Edmund Fitzgerald's* 29 crew members all perished. *Edmund Fitzgerald* adventurer Joe MacInnis reported that in July 1994, explorer Frederick Shannon's Expedition 94 to the *Fitzgerald* discovered and filmed a man's body near the port side of her pilothouse, not far from the open door, "fully clothed, wearing an orange life jacket, and lying face down in the sediment." No crew members were ever recovered. The *Fitzgerald* was swallowed up so intensely by Lake Superior that the 729-foot (222 m) ship split in half. Her two pieces are sitting approximately 170 feet (52 m) apart in a depth of 550 feet (170 m).

Storms that claimed multiple ships include the Mataafa Storm on November 28, 1905, and the Great Lakes Storm of 1913.

In August 2007 wreckage was found of the *Cyprus*, a 420-foot (130 m) ore carrier which sank during a Lake Superior storm in 460 feet (140 m) of water. All but Charles G. Pitz of the *Cyprus'* 23 crew perished on October 11, 1907. The ore carrier sank in Lake Superior on her second voyage, whilst hauling iron ore from Superior, Wisconsin, to Buffalo, New York. Built in Lorain, Ohio, the *Cyprus* was launched August 17, 1907.

Ecology

Bedrock shoreline, Neys Provincial Park, Ontario

Over 80 species of fish have been found in Lake Superior. Species native to the lake include: bloater, brook trout, burbot, cisco, lake sturgeon, lake trout, lake whitefish, longnose sucker, muskellunge, northern pike, pumpkinseed, rock bass, round whitefish, smallmouth bass, walleye, white sucker and yellow perch. In addition, many fish species have been either intentionally or accidentally introduced to Lake Superior: atlantic salmon, brown trout, carp, chinook salmon, coho salmon, freshwater drum, pink salmon, rainbow smelt, rainbow trout, round goby, ruffe, sea lamprey and white perch.

Lake Superior has fewer dissolved nutrients relative to its water volume compared to the other Great Lakes and so is less productive in terms of fish populations. This is a result of the underdeveloped soils found in its relatively small watershed. However, nitrate concentrations in the lake have been continuously rising for more than a century. They are still much lower than levels considered dangerous to human health; but this steady, long-term rise is an unusual record of environmental nitrogen buildup. It may relate to anthropogenic alternations to the regional Nitrogen Cycle, but researchers are still unsure of the causes of this change to the lake's ecology.

As for other Great Lakes fish populations have also been impacted by the accidental or intentional introduction of foreign species such as the sea lamprey and Eurasian ruffe. Accidental introductions have occurred in part by the removal of natural barriers to navigation between the Great Lakes. Overfishing has also been a factor in the decline of fish populations.

See also

- the North Shore of Lake Superior
- the South Shore of Lake Superior
- Michigan lighthouses

General

- Great Lakes
- Great Lakes Areas of Concern
- Great Lakes census statistical areas
- Great Lakes Commission
- Great Recycling and Northern Development Canal
- Great Storm of 1913
- International Boundary Waters Treaty
- List of cities along the Great Lakes
- Seiche
- Shipwrecks of the 1913 Great Lakes storm
- Sixty Years' War for control of the Great Lakes
- Third Coast

Pictured Rocks National Lakeshore, Michigan

References

Further reading

- Burt, Williams A., and Hubbard, Bela *Reports on the Mineral Region of Lake Superior* (Buffalo: L. Danforth, 1846), 113 pages [1].
- Hyde, Charles K., and Ann and John Mahan. *The Northern Lights: Lighthouses of the Upper Great Lakes.* Detroit: Wayne State University Press, 1995. ISBN 0814325548 ISBN 9780814325544.
- Oleszewski, Wes, *Great Lakes Lighthouses, American and Canadian: A Comprehensive Directory/Guide to Great Lakes Lighthouses*, (Gwinn, Michigan: Avery Color Studios, Inc., 1998) ISBN 0-932212-98-0.
- Penrod, John, *Lighthouses of Michigan*, (Berrien Center, Michigan: Penrod/Hiawatha, 1998) ISBN 9780942618785 ISBN 9781893624238
- Penrose, Laurie and Bill, A *Traveler's Guide to 116 Michigan Lighthouses* (Petoskey, Michigan: Friede Publications, 1999). ISBN 0923756035 ISBN 9780923756031
- Sims, P.K. and L.M.H. Carter, eds. *Archean and Proterozoic Geology of the Lake Superior Region, U.S.A., 1993* [U.S. Geological Survey Professional Paper 1556]. Washington, D.C.: U.S.

Department of the Interior, U.S. Geological Survey, 1996.
- Splake, T. Kilgore. *Superior Land Lights*. Battle Creek, MI: Angst Productions, 1984
- Stonehouse, Frederick. *Marquette Shipwrecks*. Marquette, MI: Harboridge Press, 1974
- Wagner, John L., *Michigan Lighthouses: An Aerial Photographic Perspective*, (East Lansing, Michigan: John L. Wagner, 1998) ISBN 1880311011 ISBN 9781880311011
- Wright, Larry and Wright, Patricia, *Great Lakes Lighthouses Encyclopedia* Hardback (Erin: Boston Mills Press, 2006) ISBN 1550463993

Shipwrecks
- "America"; Houghton, Michigan; Houghton Mining Gazette; Vol. 29; June 8, 1928
- Stonehouse, Frederick; Isle Royale Shipwrecks; Marquette, Michigan; Arery Color Studios; 1977
- "Cumberland" & "Wreck of Sidewheel Steamer Cumberland"; Detroit, Michigan; Detroit Free Press; January 29, 1974
- "S.S.George M. Cox Wrecked"; Houghton, Michigan; Houghton Mining Gazette; May 28, 1933
- Holdon, Thom "Reef of the Three C's"; Duluth, Minnesota; Lake Superior Marine Museum; Vol. 2, #4; July/August 1977
- Holdon, Thom; "Above and Below: Steamer America"; Duluth, Minnesota; Lake Superior Marine Museum; Vol. 3, #3 & #4; May/June & July/August 1978

External links
- International Lake Superior Board of Control [2]
- EPA's Great Lakes Atlas [3]
- EPA's Great Lakes Atlas Factsheet #1 [4]
- Great Lakes Coast Watch [7]
- Parks Canada Lake Superior [5]
- Minnesota Sea Grant - Lake Superior Page [6]
- Lake Superior Bathymetry [7]

pnb:جھیل سپیریئر

Cities/ Towns in Luce County

Newberry, Michigan

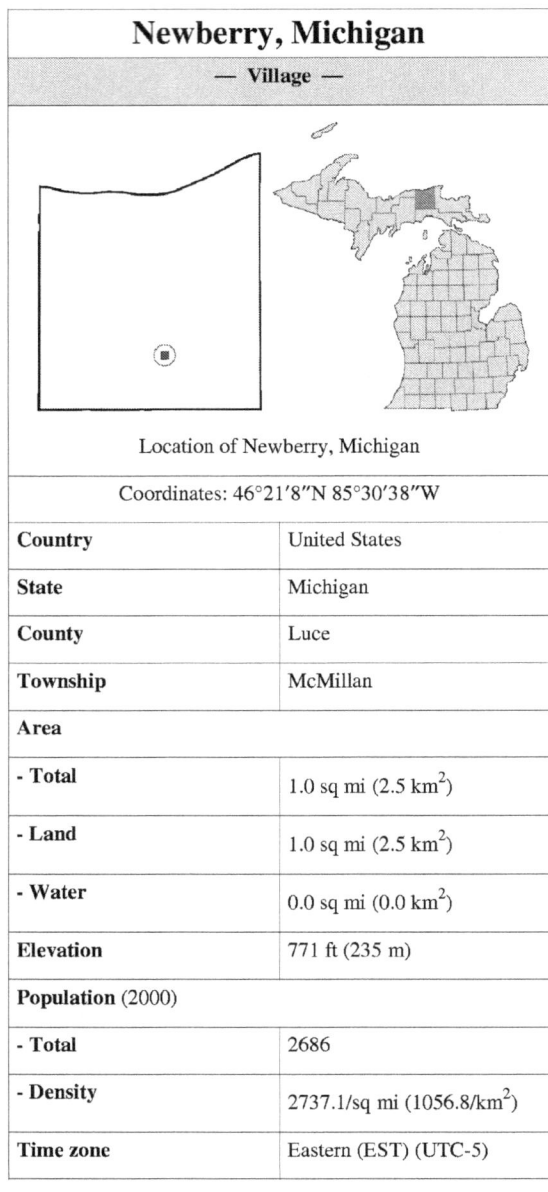

Newberry, Michigan	
— Village —	
Location of Newberry, Michigan	
Coordinates: 46°21'8"N 85°30'38"W	
Country	United States
State	Michigan
County	Luce
Township	McMillan
Area	
- Total	1.0 sq mi (2.5 km^2)
- Land	1.0 sq mi (2.5 km^2)
- Water	0.0 sq mi (0.0 km^2)
Elevation	771 ft (235 m)
Population (2000)	
- Total	2686
- Density	2737.1/sq mi (1056.8/km^2)
Time zone	Eastern (EST) (UTC-5)

- Summer (DST)	EDT (UTC-4)
ZIP code	49868
Area code(s)	906
FIPS code	26-57140
GNIS feature ID	0633350

Newberry is a village in the U.S. state of Michigan and the county seat of Luce County. Located within McMillan Township at its very southern end, it shares some administrative responsibilities with the surrounding township. The population was 2,686 at the 2000 census.

The village was named in honor of John Stoughton Newberry, a U.S. Representative and industrialist from the state of Michigan.

Newberry is surrounded by miles of state and national forests and is considered one of two gateways to the Tahquamenon Falls area. (The other is Paradise, approximately 40 miles to the northeast.) Newberry was designated as the moose capital of Michigan by the state legislature, in House Resolution 2002-572 and Senate Resolution 2002-259. It is home to the Newberry Correctional Facility, operating since 1996.

In August 2007, the Sleeper Lakes Fire burned for several weeks north of Newberry, and firefighting efforts were coordinated from this village.

The Newberry High School football team competes each year for the Little Brown Jug of the Upper Peninsula of Michigan, a rivalry game with Sault Sainte Marie dating back to 1913.

Geography

According to the United States Census Bureau, the village has a total area of 1.0 square miles (2.5 km²), all land.

Transportation

- M-28 travels west to Marquette and east to Sault Ste. Marie.
- M-123 runs northerly and northeasterly from Newberry to Tahquamenon Falls State Park and Paradise.

Demographics

Historic preservationists lost the 1970s fight to save the county's elaborate courthouse, but managed to keep the elaborate sheriff's house, now the Luce County Historical Museum.

As of the census of 2000, there were 2,686 people, 717 households, and 456 families residing in the village. The population density was 2,737.1 per square mile (1,058.2/km²). There were 824 housing units at an average density of 839.7/sq mi (324.6/km²). The racial makeup of the village was 69.92% White, 19.29% African American, 4.95% Native American, 0.67% Asian, 0.04% Pacific Islander, 1.01% from other races, and 4.13% from two or more races. Hispanic or Latino of any race were 3.69% of the population.

The Luce County Historical Museum is housed in the historic, 1894 sheriff's house and county jail. In the 1970s, historic preservationists lost a fight to preserve county's elaborate courthouse; however its fountain was moved to the front of the museum.

There were 717 households of which 32.6% had children under the age of 18 living with them, 46.7% were married couples living together, 12.4% had a female householder with no husband present, and 36.4% were non-families. 32.5% of all households were made up of individuals and 18.0% had someone living alone who was 65 years of age or older. The average household size was 2.36 and the average family size was 2.95.

In the village the population was spread out with 18.2% under the age of 18, 12.5% from 18 to 24, 39.4% from 25 to 44, 16.4% from 45 to 64, and 13.6% who were 65 years of age or older. The median age was 34 years. For every 100 females there were 181.0 males. For every 100 females age 18 and over, there were 215.7 males.

The median income for a household in the village was $29,052, and the median income for a family was $36,607. Males had a median income of $29,286 versus $20,956 for females. The per capita income for the village was $17,224. About 15.6% of families and 18.1% of the population were below the poverty line, including 27.5% of those under age 18 and 8.4% of those age 65 or over.

Media

In addition to two radio stations broadcasting directly from Newberry, radio stations from the Sault Ste. Marie market can also be heard in the community.

- 93.9 FM - WNBY (Oldies)
- 97.9 FM - WIHC (classic rock)
- 96.7 FM - The Eagle ("We Play Everything")

Luce County Government Building

Notable natives

- Terry O'Quinn, who plays John Locke (Lost) on Lost, is from Newberry.
- Rob Rubick, former Detroit Lion and analyst for Fox Sports Net Detroit, is from Newberry.
- Len St. Jean, a former Boston Patriot, is from Newberry.

External links

- Newberry Area Chamber of Commerce [1]
- Newberry Area Tourism Association [2]

McMillan Township Hall

- House Journal containing HR 572 designating Newberry as Moose Capital of Michigan [3]
- Senate Journal containing SR 259 designating Newberry as Moose Capital of Michigan [4]
- Newberry Correctional Facility [5]
- Newberry Michigan Homepage For Locals [6]

Geographical coordinates: 46°21'18"N 85°30'34"W

Columbus Township, Luce County, Michigan

Columbus Township, Michigan	
— Township —	
Columbus Township, Michigan Location within the state of Michigan	
Coordinates: 46°24′54″N 85°44′52″W	
Country	United States
State	Michigan
County	Luce
Area	
- Total	143.3 sq mi (371.1 km^2)
- Land	140.8 sq mi (364.6 km^2)
- Water	2.5 sq mi (6.5 km^2)
Elevation	863 ft (263 m)
Population (2000)	
- Total	215
- Density	1.5/sq mi (0.6/km^2)
Time zone	Eastern (EST) (UTC-5)
- Summer (DST)	EDT (UTC-4)
FIPS code	26-17480

Columbus Township, Luce County, Michigan

| GNIS feature ID | 1626122 |

Columbus Township is a civil township of Luce County in the U.S. state of Michigan. As of the 2000 census, the township population was 215.

Communities

- **Danaher** is an unincorporated community at 46°20′37″N 85°46′51″W just north of M-28 west of Newberry.
- **Laketon** is an unincorporated community at 46°20′34″N 85°44′54″W, approximately 3 miles (4.8 km) west of McMillan. Laketon was a whistlestop on the Duluth, South Shore and Atlantic Railroad. A post office opened on March 11, 1902, with John M. Carr as its first postmaster. The office closed on May 15, 1913.
- **McMillan** is an unincorporated community at 46°20′20″N 85°41′14″W. The settlement began when the Duluth, South Shore and Atlantic Railroad was built through here in 1881. The station was named for James McMillan, then an executive of the railroad and future U.S. Senator from Michigan. McMillan's colleague in the railroad company, John Stoughton Newberry, is the namesake of the village of Newberry, approximately 10 miles (16 km) to the east. A post office was established on April 21, 1882, and the Mc Millan post office, with ZIP code 49853 serves central Columbus Township as well as much of Lakefield Township to the south and smaller portions of McMillan Township, to the east, and Portage Township to the south of Lakefield in Mackinac County.

Geography

According to the United States Census Bureau, the township has a total area of 143.3 square miles (371.1 km²), of which, 140.8 square miles (364.6 km²) of it is land and 2.5 square miles (6.4 km²) of it (1.74%) is water.

Demographics

As of the census of 2000, there were 215 people, 99 households, and 63 families residing in the township. The population density was 1.5 per square mile (0.6/km²). There were 307 housing units at an average density of 2.2/sq mi (0.8/km²). The racial makeup of the township was 96.28% White, 1.40% Native American, and 2.33% from two or more races. Hispanic or Latino of any race were 0.47% of the population.

There were 99 households out of which 21.2% had children under the age of 18 living with them, 54.5% were married couples living together, 2.0% had a female householder with no husband present, and 35.4% were non-families. 31.3% of all households were made up of individuals and 12.1% had someone living alone who was 65 years of age or older. The average household size was 2.17 and the average family size was 2.72.

In the township the population was spread out with 21.4% under the age of 18, 4.2% from 18 to 24, 23.3% from 25 to 44, 36.7% from 45 to 64, and 14.4% who were 65 years of age or older. The median age was 46 years. For every 100 females there were 102.8 males. For every 100 females age 18 and over, there were 96.5 males.

The median income for a household in the township was $30,469, and the median income for a family was $33,750. Males had a median income of $32,813 versus $20,000 for females. The per capita income for the township was $18,289. About 8.3% of families and 12.9% of the population were below the poverty line, including 20.5% of those under the age of eighteen and 25.0% of those sixty five or over.

Lakefield Township, Luce County, Michigan

Lakefield Township, Michigan	
— Township —	
Lakefield Township, Michigan Location within the state of Michigan	
Coordinates: 46°16′38″N 85°42′55″W	
Country	United States
State	Michigan
County	Luce
Area	
- Total	72.1 sq mi (186.6 km^2)
- Land	63.4 sq mi (164.1 km^2)
- Water	8.7 sq mi (22.5 km^2)
Elevation	712 ft (217 m)
Population (2000)	
- Total	1074
- Density	16.9/sq mi (6.5/km^2)
Time zone	Eastern (EST) (UTC-5)
- Summer (DST)	EDT (UTC-4)
FIPS code	26-44540

Lakefield Township, Luce County, Michigan

| GNIS feature ID | 1626582 |

Lakefield Township is a civil township of Luce County in the U.S. state of Michigan. The population was 1,074 at the 2000 census.

Communities

- Helmer is an unincorporated community on at the northeast shore of Mantistique Lake and the location of the historic Helmer House Inn.
- **Carpenter Landing** is an unincorporated community at 46°17′23″N 85°45′28″W on the western shore of North Manistique Lake and southwest of Newberry.

Geography

According to the United States Census Bureau, the township has a total area of 72.1 square miles (186.6 km²), of which, 63.4 square miles (164.1 km²) of it is land and 8.7 square miles (22.5 km²) of it (12.07%) is water.

Demographics

As of the census of 2000, there were 1,074 people, 449 households, and 347 families residing in the township. The population density was 16.9 per square mile (6.5/km²). There were 897 housing units at an average density of 14.2/sq mi (5.5/km²). The racial makeup of the township was 94.13% White, 0.09% African American, 2.98% Native American, 0.47% Asian, 0.09% Pacific Islander, 0.09% from other races, and 2.14% from two or more races. Hispanic or Latino of any race were 0.19% of the population.

There were 449 households out of which 22.9% had children under the age of 18 living with them, 71.0% were married couples living together, 4.5% had a female householder with no husband present, and 22.7% were non-families. 19.4% of all households were made up of individuals and 7.1% had someone living alone who was 65 years of age or older. The average household size was 2.37 and the average family size was 2.68.

In the township the population was spread out with 19.4% under the age of 18, 4.6% from 18 to 24, 20.8% from 25 to 44, 35.6% from 45 to 64, and 19.7% who were 65 years of age or older. The median age was 48 years. For every 100 females there were 104.6 males. For every 100 females age 18 and over, there were 102.8 males.

The median income for a household in the township was $34,773, and the median income for a family was $38,472. Males had a median income of $32,596 versus $20,536 for females. The per capita income for the township was $16,671. About 6.4% of families and 11.2% of the population were below the poverty line, including 21.1% of those under age 18 and 2.4% of those age 65 or over.

McMillan Township, Luce County, Michigan

McMillan Township, Michigan
— Township —

McMillan Township Hall, Newberry

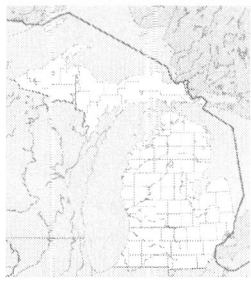

McMillan Township, Michigan
Location within the state of Michigan

Coordinates: 46°32'16"N 85°30'13"W

Country	United States
State	Michigan
County	Luce
Area	
- Total	604.6 sq mi (1566.0 km^2)
- Land	592.0 sq mi (1533.4 km^2)

- Water	12.6 sq mi (32.6 km^2)
Elevation	804 ft (245 m)
Population (2000)	
- Total	3947
- Density	6.7/sq mi (2.6/km^2)
Time zone	Eastern (EST) (UTC-5)
- Summer (DST)	EDT (UTC-4)
ZIP code	49768, 49853, 49868
Area code(s)	906
FIPS code	26-50440
GNIS feature ID	1626658

McMillan Township is a civil township of northern Luce County in the U.S. state of Michigan. The population was 3,947 at the 2000 census. Most of the township's population lives in the village of Newberry, the county seat, at the township's extreme south.

Communities

- **Betty B Landing** [formerly **Hunter's Landing**] is classified as a populated place by the United States Geological Survey located at 46°24′02″N 85°16′40″W on the Tahquamenon River. The landing is the northern terminus of a private railroad spur from Soo Junction, which now operates as the Toonerville Trolley Riverboat Tour offering tours on the 5.5 miles (8.9 km) 24-inch gauge railroad. The branch was built by the Duluth, South Shore and Atlantic Railroad from Soo Junction to the Hunter & Love Lumber Company mill on the Tahquamenon River in 1911. Built in standard gauge, the line was converted to narrow gauge to accommodate the mining engines used to pull the trolley tour's cars by Joseph Beech, Sr., founder of the riverboat tours.
- **Deer Park** is a former lumbering settlement in the township.
- Dollarville is an unincorporated community just west of Newberry.
- Newberry is a village on M-123. It is the county seat and the main population center in both the township and county.

Geography

According to the United States Census Bureau, the township has a total area of 604.6 square miles (1,566.0 km²), of which 592.0 square miles (1,533.4 km²) is land and 12.6 square miles (32.6 km² or 2.08%) is water. It is the largest township in Michigan.

Demographics

As of the census of 2000, there were 3,947 people, 1,240 households, and 813 families residing in the township. The population density was 6.7 per square mile (2.6/km²). There were 1,979 housing units at an average density of 3.3/sq mi (1.3/km²). The racial makeup of the township was 76.39% White, 13.28% African American, 5.60% Native American, 0.46% Asian, 0.03% Pacific Islander, 0.79% from other races, and 3.47% from two or more races. Hispanic or Latino of any race were 2.86% of the population.

There were 1,240 households out of which 30.7% had children under the age of 18 living with them, 50.9% were married couples living together, 10.6% had a female householder with no husband present, and 34.4% were non-families. 30.8% of all households were made up of individuals and 15.3% had someone living alone who was 65 years of age or older. The average household size was 2.35 and the average family size was 2.89.

In the township the population was spread out with 19.7% under the age of 18, 10.8% from 18 to 24, 34.9% from 25 to 44, 20.1% from 45 to 64, and 14.5% who were 65 years of age or older. The median age was 36 years. For every 100 females there were 146.2 males. For every 100 females age 18 and over, there were 165.0 males.

The median income for a household in the township was $30,514, and the median income for a family was $35,101. Males had a median income of $30,118 versus $20,608 for females. The per capita income for the township was $17,007. About 14.6% of families and 16.9% of the population were below the poverty line, including 19.8% of those under age 18 and 9.7% of those age 65 or over.

Pentland Township, Michigan

Pentland Township, Michigan	
— Township —	
Pentland Township, Michigan Location within the state of Michigan	
Coordinates: 46°18′0″N 85°29′16″W	
Country	United States
State	Michigan
County	Luce
Area	
- Total	107.3 sq mi (278.0 km²)
- Land	106.9 sq mi (276.9 km²)
- Water	0.4 sq mi (1.1 km²)
Elevation	801 ft (244 m)
Population (2000)	
- Total	1788
- Density	16.7/sq mi (6.5/km²)
Time zone	Eastern (EST) (UTC-5)
- Summer (DST)	EDT (UTC-4)
FIPS code	26-63500
GNIS feature ID	1626892

Pentland Township is a civil township of Luce County in the U.S. state of Michigan. As of the 2000 census, the township population was 1,788.

Geography

According to the United States Census Bureau, the township has a total area of 107.3 square miles (278.0 km²), of which, 106.9 square miles (276.9 km²) of it is land and 0.4 square miles (1.1 km²) of it (0.40%) is water.

Demographics

As of the census of 2000, there were 1,788 people, 693 households, and 516 families residing in the township. The population density was 16.7 per square mile (6.5/km²). There were 825 housing units at an average density of 7.7/sq mi (3.0/km²). The racial makeup of the township was 88.70% White, 0.17% African American, 7.44% Native American, 0.11% Asian, 0.06% from other races, and 3.52% from two or more races. Hispanic or Latino of any race were 0.39% of the population.

There were 693 households out of which 32.8% had children under the age of 18 living with them, 62.3% were married couples living together, 8.4% had a female householder with no husband present, and 25.5% were non-families. 21.9% of all households were made up of individuals and 9.7% had someone living alone who was 65 years of age or older. The average household size was 2.55 and the average family size was 2.95.

In the township the population was spread out with 26.4% under the age of 18, 6.5% from 18 to 24, 27.6% from 25 to 44, 24.6% from 45 to 64, and 14.9% who were 65 years of age or older. The median age was 39 years. For every 100 females there were 100.4 males. For every 100 females age 18 and over, there were 98.8 males.

The median income for a household in the township was $35,990, and the median income for a family was $37,991. Males had a median income of $34,583 versus $22,692 for females. The per capita income for the township was $16,352. About 12.0% of families and 14.0% of the population were below the poverty line, including 20.3% of those under age 18 and 8.6% of those age 65 or over.

Nearby Counties

Alger County, Michigan

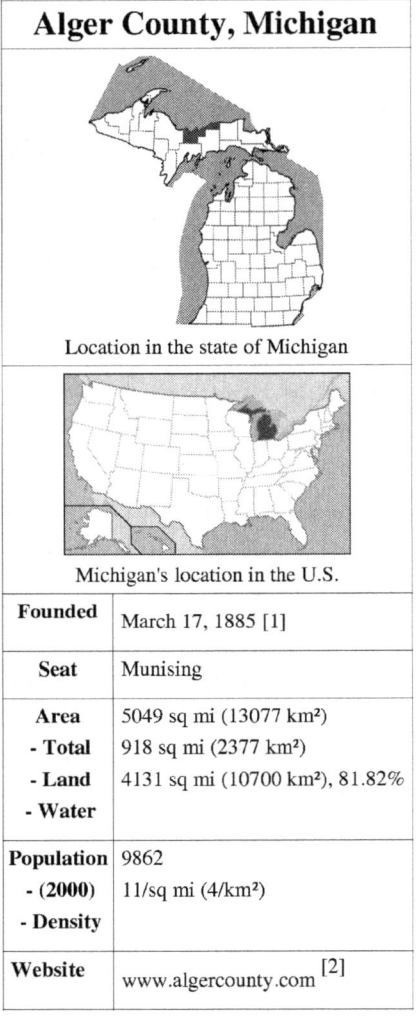

Alger County, Michigan	
Founded	March 17, 1885 [1]
Seat	Munising
Area - Total - Land - Water	5049 sq mi (13077 km²) 918 sq mi (2377 km²) 4131 sq mi (10700 km²), 81.82%
Population - (2000) - Density	9862 11/sq mi (4/km²)
Website	www.algercounty.com [2]

Alger County is a county in the U.S. state of Michigan. As of the 2000 census, the population was 9,862. Its county seat is Munising. The Pictured Rocks National Lakeshore is located within the county.

History

Alger County was detached from Schoolcraft County, set off and organized in 1885. The county was named for lumber baron Russell Alexander Alger who was a Michigan Governor, U.S. Senator and U.S. Secretary of War during the William McKinley Presidential administration. *See also*, List of Michigan county name etymologies, List of Michigan counties, and List of abolished U.S. counties.

Alger County Courthouse Complex, Munising

Geography

According to the U.S. Census Bureau, the county has a total area of 5049 square miles (13080 km^2), of which 918 square miles (2380 km^2) is land and 4131 square miles (10700 km^2) (81.82%) is water.

Highways

US Highways

- [41] US 41

Michigan State Trunklines

- M-28
- M-67
- M-77
- M-94

County-Designated Highways

- H-01
- H-03
- H-05
- H-11
- H-13, also designated Federal Forest Highway 13.
- H-15
- H-44
- H-52
- H-58, passes through Pictured Rocks National Lakeshore.

The Midway General Store on FFH-13 in southern Alger County

Federal Forest Highways

- Federal Forest Highway 13 (FFH-13)

Adjacent counties

- Luce County (east)
- Schoolcraft County (southeast)
- Delta County (south)
- Marquette County (west)
- Thunder Bay District, Ontario (north, water boundary only, in Lake Superior)

National protected areas

- Grand Island National Recreation Area
- Hiawatha National Forest (part)
- Pictured Rocks National Lakeshore

Demographics

Bridalveil Falls emptying into Lake Superior

As of the 2000 census, there were 9,862 people, 3,785 households, and 2,585 families residing in the county. The population density was 11 people per square mile (4/km²). There were 5,964 housing units at an average density of 6 per square mile (3/km²). The racial makeup of the county was 87.81% White, 6.11% Black or African American, 3.30% Native American, 0.32% Asian, 0.04% Pacific Islander, 0.39% from other races, and 2.03% from two or more races. 1.00% of the population were Hispanic or Latino of any race. 14.9% were of Finnish, 11.7% German, 9.5% French, 7.5% Polish, 6.5% American, 6.1% English, 5.9% Irish, 5.7% French Canadian and 5.1% Swedish ancestry according to Census 2000. 95.5% spoke English, 2.1% Finnish and 1.7% Spanish as their first language.

There were 3,785 households out of which 27.00% had children under the age of 18 living with them, 57.00% were married couples living together, 7.60% had a female householder with no husband present, and 31.70% were non-families. 26.80% of all households were made up of individuals and 12.60% had someone living alone who was 65 years of age or older. The average household size was 2.35 and the average family size was 2.83.

In the county the population was spread out with 20.50% under the age of 18, 7.30% from 18 to 24, 28.70% from 25 to 44, 26.30% from 45 to 64, and 17.20% who were 65 years of age or older. The median age was 41 years. For every 100 females there were 116.60 males. For every 100 females age 18 and over, there were 120.60 males.

The median income for a household in the county was $35,892, and the median income for a family was $42,017. Males had a median income of $37,681 versus $24,492 for females. The per capita income for the county was $18,210. About 7.20% of families and 10.30% of the population were below the poverty line, including 12.70% of those under age 18 and 8.10% of those age 65 or over.

Government

The county government operates the jail, maintains rural roads, operates the major local courts, keeps files of deeds and mortgages, maintains vital records, administers public health regulations, and participates with the state in the provision of welfare and other social services. The county board of commissioners controls the budget but has only limited authority to make laws or ordinances. In Michigan, most local government functions — police and fire, building and zoning, tax assessment, street maintenance, etc. — are the responsibility of individual cities and townships.

Alger County elected officials

(information as of August 2007)

- Prosecuting Attorney: Karen Bahrman
- Sheriff: David M. Cromell
- County Clerk/Register of Deeds: Mary Ann Froberg
- County Treasurer: Howard Masters
- Commissioner, District 1: Catherine Pullen (chair)
- Commissioner, District 2: Todd Brock
- Commissioner, District 3: Esley Mattson
- Commissioner, District 4: Donald Sandstrom
- Commissioner, District 5: Edward Lindstrom

Cities, villages, and townships

Cities
- Munising

Villages
- Chatham

Unincorporated communities

- Au Train
- Christmas
- Coalwood
- Deerton
- Diffin
- Dixon
- Dorsey
- Doty
- Eben Junction
- Evelyn
- Grand Marais
- Green Haven
- Indian Town
- Juniper
- Kentucky
- Kiva
- Ladoga
- Limestone
- Melstrand
- Munising Junction
- Myren
- Rumely
- Shingleton
- Slapneck
- Star
- Stillman
- Sundell
- Traunik
- Trenary
- Vail
- Van Meer
- Wetmore

Townships

- Au Train Township
- Burt Township
- Grand Island Township
- Limestone Township
- Mathias Township
- Munising Township
- Onota Township
- Rock River Township

External links

- Alger County Online [3]
- Munising Area Partnership for Development, Inc. [4]
- National Association of Counties - Alger County, MI [5]

Geographical coordinates: 47°10′N 86°29′W

Chippewa County, Michigan

Chippewa County, Michigan	
Logo	
 Location in the state of Michigan	
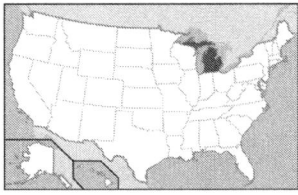 Michigan's location in the U.S.	
Founded	1826
Seat	Sault Ste. Marie
Largest city	Sault Ste. Marie
Area - Total - Land - Water	2698 sq mi (6988 km²) 1561 sq mi (4043 km²) 1137 sq mi (2945 km²), 42.14%
Population - (2000) - Density	38543 26/sq mi (10/km²)
Website	www.chippewacountymi.gov [1]

Chippewa County, Michigan

Chippewa County is a county in the Upper Peninsula of the U.S. state of Michigan. As of the 2000 census, the population was 38,543. The county seat is Sault Ste. Marie.

Geography

Chippewa County Courthouse, Sault Ste. Marie

- According to the U.S. Census Bureau, the county has a total area of 2698 square miles (6987.8 km^2), of which 1561 square miles (4043.0 km^2) is land and 1137 square miles (2944.8 km^2) (42.14%) is water.
- The Michigan Meridian runs through the eastern portion of the county. South of Nine Mile Road, M-129 (Meridian Road) overlays the meridian. In Sault Ste. Marie, Meridian Street north of 12th Avenue overlays the meridian.

Transportation

Michigan State Trunklines

All Interstate and US Highways in MIchigan, like all state-maintained highways, are part of the Michigan State Trunkline Highway System.

Chippewa County, Michigan from 1904 Michigan County Maps

- I-75 ends at the Sault Ste. Marie International Bridge at the Canada border.
- M-28
- M-48
- M-80
- M-123
- M-129
- M-134
- M-221
- BS I-75 travels from I-75 into downtown Sault Ste. Marie.

Chippewa County-Designated Highways

The following highways are maintained by the Chippewa County Road Commission as part of the county road system. They are assigned numbers by the Michigan Department of Transportation as part of the County-Designated Highway System.

- H-40
- H-63 runs via Mackinac Trail, the former route of US 2 before it was replaced by I-75 in 1962.

Adjacent counties

- Algoma District, Ontario, Canada (northeast, east)
- Manitoulin District, Ontario, Canada (east)
- Presque Isle County (southeast, water boundary only, in Lake Huron)
- Mackinac County (south)
- Luce County (west)

National protected areas

- Harbor Island National Wildlife Refuge
- Hiawatha National Forest (part)
- Whitefish Point Unit of the Seney National Wildlife Refuge

Demographics

As of the census of 2000, there were 38,543 people, 13,474 households, and 8,960 families residing in the county. The population density was 25 people per square mile (10/km²). There were 19,430 housing units at an average density of 12 per square mile (5/km²). The racial makeup of the county was 75.88% White, 5.52% Black or African American, 13.31% Native American, 0.46% Asian, 0.03% Pacific Islander, 0.37% from other races, and 4.43% from two or more races. 1.55% of the population were Hispanic or Latino of any race. 14.9% were of German, 9.8% English, 9.0% Irish, 7.4% French and 6.0% Polish ancestry. 95.3% spoke English and 1.7% Spanish as their first language.

There were 13,474 households out of which 30.40% had children under the age of 18 living with them, 51.50% were married couples living together, 10.70% had a female householder with no husband present, and 33.50% were non-families. 27.50% of all households were made up of individuals and 10.70% had someone living alone who was 65 years of age or older. The average household size was 2.42 and the average family size was 2.93.

In the county the population was spread out with 21.30% under the age of 18, 11.90% from 18 to 24, 31.80% from 25 to 44, 22.30% from 45 to 64, and 12.70% who were 65 years of age or older. The median age was 36 years. For every 100 females there were 125.50 males. For every 100 females age 18 and over, there were 132.10 males.

The median income for a household in the county was $34,464, and the median income for a family was $41,450. Males had a median income of $31,559 versus $22,321 for females. The per capita income for the county was $15,858. About 8.90% of families and 12.80% of the population were below the poverty line, including 15.60% of those under age 18 and 9.60% of those age 65 or over.

Government

The county government operates the jail, maintains rural roads, operates the major local courts, keeps files of deeds and mortgages, maintains vital records, administers public health regulations, and participates with the state in the provision of welfare and other social services. The county board of commissioners controls the budget but has only limited authority to make laws or ordinances. In Michigan, most local government functions — police and fire, building and zoning, tax assessment, street maintenance, etc. — are the responsibility of individual cities and townships.

Chippewa County elected officials

- Prosecuting Attorney: Brian Peppler
- Sheriff: Robert Savoie
- County Clerk: Diane Cork
- County Treasurer: Marilyn McDonald
- Register of Deeds: Sharon Kennedy
- Drain Commissioner: Anthony Bosley
- County Surveyor: William Karr

(information updated July 2010)

Cities, villages, and townships

Cities

- Sault Ste. Marie

Villages

- De Tour Village

Unincorporated communities

- Barbeau
- Bay Mills
- Bay Mills Indian Community
- Brimley
- Dafter
- Drummond
- Keldon
- Kincheloe
- Paradise
- Pickford
- Rudyard
- Stirlingville

Townships

- Bay Mills Township
- Bruce Township
- Chippewa Township
- Dafter Township
- Detour Township
- Drummond Township
- Hulbert Township
- Kinross Charter Township
- Pickford Township
- Raber Township
- Rudyard Township
- Soo Township
- Sugar Island Township
- Superior Township
- Trout Lake Township
- Whitefish Township

See also

- Delirium Wilderness

External links

- Chippewa County Government [2]
- Clarke Historical Library, Central, Michigan University, Bibliography for Chippewa County [3]

Geographical coordinates: 46°19′N 84°31′W

Mackinac County, Michigan

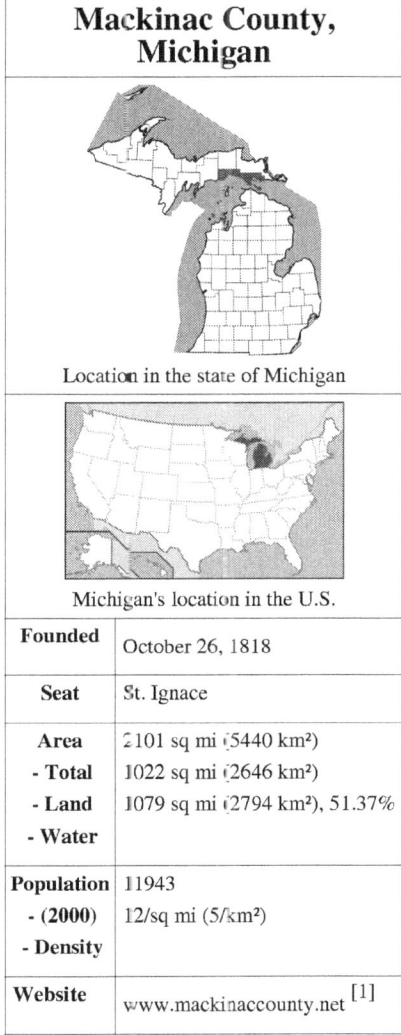

Mackinac County, Michigan	
Founded	October 26, 1818
Seat	St. Ignace
Area - Total - Land - Water	2101 sq mi (5440 km²) 1022 sq mi (2646 km²) 1079 sq mi (2794 km²), 51.37%
Population - (2000) - Density	11943 12/sq mi (5/km²)
Website	www.mackinaccounty.net [1]

Mackinac County is a county in the Upper Peninsula of the U.S. state of Michigan. As of the 2000 census, the population was 11,943. The county seat is St. Ignace. The county was formerly known as **Michilimackinac County**, and it was created as one of the first counties of the Michigan Territory in 1818.

The county's name is claimed to be a corruption of the French term "Michilimackinac," which referred to the straits area as well as the French settlement at the tip of the lower peninsula. *See and compare* List of Michigan county name etymologies, List of Michigan counties, and List of abolished U.S. counties.

History

Michilimackinac County was created on October 26, 1818 by proclamation of territorial governor Lewis Cass. The county originally took up the Lower Peninsula of Michigan north of Macomb County and almost the entire present Upper Peninsula. At the time of founding, the county seat was the community of Michilimackinac Island on Michilimackinac Island, later known as Mackinac Island, Michigan. The county was reorganized in 1849 as Mackinac County. In 1882 the county seat was moved from Mackinac Island to St. Ignace.

Geography

- According to the U.S. Census Bureau, the county has a total area of 2,101 square miles (5,440 km²), of which, 1,022 square miles (2,646 km²) of it is land and 1,079 square miles (2,794 km²) of it (51.37%) is water.
- It is part of the Roman Catholic Diocese of Marquette.
- St. Ignace is the northern terminus of the Mackinac Bridge.
- Mackinac Island is within the county.

Adjacent counties

- Chippewa (northeast, east)
- Presque Isle County (southeast, water boundary only, in Lake Huron)
- Cheboygan County (south, water boundary only, in Lake Huron)
- Emmet County (south, water boundary only, in Lake Michigan)
- Charlevoix County (southwest, water boundary only, in Lake Michigan)
- Schoolcraft County (west)
- Luce County (northwest)

National protected area

- Hiawatha National Forest (part)

Transportation

Private Airports

- Mackinac County Airport (St. Ignace)
- Mackinac Island Airport (Mackinac Island)

Airline service

The nearest airports with scheduled passenger service are:

Mackinac County, Michigan

- Chippewa County International Airport in Sault Ste Marie in the eastern Upper peninsula;
- Pellston Regional Airport, Traverse City Cherry Capital Airport and Alpena County Regional Airport in the Lower Peninsula.

Interstates

- I-75

Interstate Business Loops

- BL I-75 runs through downtown St. Ignace

US Highways

- US 2

Michigan State Trunklines

- M-48
- M-117
- M-123
- M-129
- M-134
- M-185, no motor vehicles allowed with the exception of emergency vehicles

Mackinac County-Designated Highways

- H-33
- H-40
- H-42
- H-57
- H-63

Ferry

Numerous companies operate ferries to Bois Blanc Island and Mackinac Island. Ferries to and from Mackinac Island sail from St. Ignace and Mackinaw City, while the Bois Blanc Island ferry sails from Cheboygan.

Rail

- Soo Line Railroad

Demographics

As of the census of 2000, there were 11,943 people, 5,067 households, and 3,410 families residing in the county. The population density was 12 persons per square mile (5/km²). There were 9,413 housing units at an average density of 9/sq mi (4/km²). The racial makeup of the county was 80.07% White, 0.20% Black or African American, 14.21% Native American, 0.31% Asian, 0.02% Pacific Islander, 0.28% from other races, and 4.92% from two or more races. 0.90% of the population were Hispanic or Latino of any race. 18.7% were of German, 9.4% English, 8.1% Irish, 7.3% French, 6.0% American and 6.0% Polish ancestry according to Census 2000. 97.6% spoke English as their first language.

There were 5,067 households out of which 26.50% had children under the age of 18 living with them, 55.60% were married couples living together, 8.10% had a female householder with no husband present, and 32.70% were non-families. 28.00% of all households were made up of individuals and 11.90% had someone living alone who was 65 years of age or older. The average household size was 2.32 and the average family size was 2.81.

In the county the population was spread out with 22.20% under the age of 18, 6.00% from 18 to 24, 25.10% from 25 to 44, 28.40% from 45 to 64, and 18.20% who were 65 years of age or older. The median age was 43 years. For every 100 females there were 99.70 males. For every 100 females age 18 and over, there were 97.20 males.

The median income for a household in the county was $33,356, and the median income for a family was $39,929. Males had a median income of $30,805 versus $22,753 for females. The per capita income for the county was $17,777. About 7.20% of families and 10.50% of the population were below the poverty line, including 13.70% of those under age 18 and 8.40% of those age 65 or over.

Government

The county government operates the jail, maintains rural roads, operates the major local courts, keeps files of deeds and mortgages, maintains vital records, administers public health regulations, and participates with the state in the provision of welfare and other social services. The county board of commissioners controls the budget but has only limited authority to make laws or ordinances. In Michigan, most local government functions — police and fire, building and zoning, tax assessment, street maintenance, etc. — are the responsibility of individual cities and townships.

Mackinac County elected officials

- Prosecuting Attorney: Alfred E. Feleppa
- Sheriff: Scott Strait
- County Clerk: Mary Kay Tamlyn
- County Treasurer: Nora A. Massey
- Register of Deeds: Diane Frankovich
- County Surveyor: Jeffrey M. Davis

(information as of September 2005)

Historical markers

There are 34 official state historical markers in the County:

- Across the Peninsula
- American Fur Company Store
- Battlefield of 1814
- Biddle House
- Bois Blanc Island
- British Cannon
- British Landing
- Early Missionary Bark Chapel
- Epoufette
- Fort de Buade
- Fort Holmes
- Grand Hotel
- Gros Cap Island & St. Helena Island
- Historic Fort Mackinac
- Indian Dormitory
- Island House (Mackinac Island)
- Lake Michigan
- Lake View Hotel
- Little Stone Church
- Mackinac Conference
- Mackinac Island
- Mackinac Straits
- Market Street
- Mission Church

- Mission House
- Northernmost Point of Lake Michigan
- Old Agency House
- Round Island Lighthouse
- Sainte Anne Church
- St. Ignace
- St. Ignace Mission
- Skull Cave
- Trinity Church (Mackinac Island)
- Wawashkamo Golf Club

Cities, villages, and townships

Cities

- Mackinac Island
- St. Ignace

Villages

- *None*

Unincorporated communities

- Allenville
- Brevort
- Cedarville
- Curtis
- Engadine
- Epoufette
- Evergreen Shores
- Garnet
- Gould City
- Gros Cap
- Hessel
- Millecoquins
- Moran
- Naubinway
- Pointe Aux Pins
- Rexton

Townships

- Bois Blanc Township
- Brevort Township
- Clark Township
- Garfield Township
- Hendricks Township
- Hudson Township
- Marquette Township
- Moran Township
- Newton Township
- Portage Township
- St. Ignace Township

Media

Newspapers

- The *Mackinac Island Town Crier* is the weekly seasonal newspaper of Mackinac Island.
- The *St. Ignace News* is the weekly newspaper for the Upper Peninsula area of the Mackinac Straits.

Television

The following television stations can be received in St. Ignace:

- Channel 4: WTOM-TV "TV 7&4" (NBC) (Cheboygan) (simulcasted in Channel 7, Harrietta)
- Channel 8: WGTQ "ABC 29&8" (ABC) (Goetzville) (simulcasted in Channel 29, Kalkaska)
- Channel 10: WWUP-TV "9&10 News" (CBS) (Goetzville) (simulcasted in Channel 9, Tustin)

Radio

The following stations can be heard in St. Ignace:

FM

Call Sign	Frequency	City Broadcast From
WIAB	88.5	Mackinaw City
WLJZ	94.5	Mackinaw City
WLXT	96.3	Petoskey
WKLZ	98.9	Petoskey
WMKC	102.9	Indian River
WCMW	103.9	Harbor Springs
WKHQ	105.9	Petoskey

AM

Call Sign	Frequency	City Broadcast From
WTCM	580	Traverse City
WARD	750	Petoskey
WIDG	940	St Ignace
WJML	1100	Petoskey
WCBY	1240	Cheboygan

Attractions

- Beaches
- Garlyn Zoo
- Lake Michigan

Bibliography

- Clarke Historical Library, Central Michigan University, Bibliography on Mackinac County. [2]

External links

- Mackinac County government [1]
- A History of the Upper Peninsula of Michigan, Fuller, George N. [3]
- St. Ignace visitor's bureau [4]

Geographical coordinates: 46°01′N 85°01′W

Schoolcraft County, Michigan

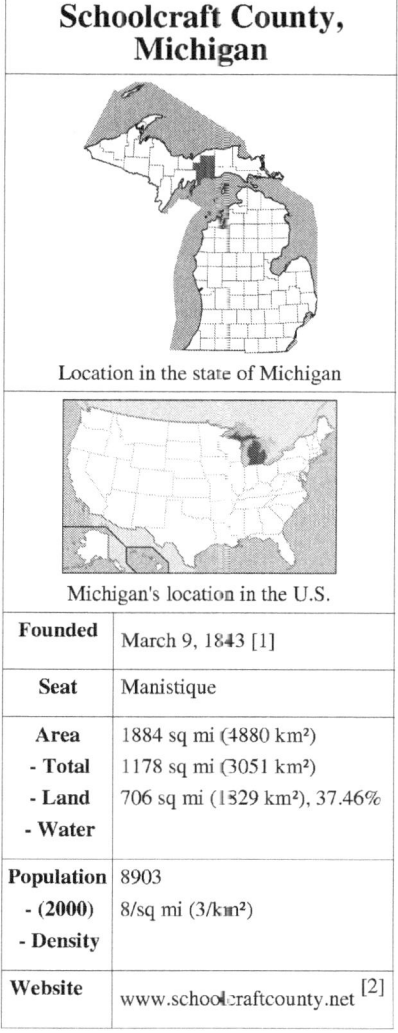

Schoolcraft County, Michigan	
Location in the state of Michigan	
Michigan's location in the U.S.	
Founded	March 9, 1843 [1]
Seat	Manistique
Area - Total - Land - Water	1884 sq mi (4880 km²) 1178 sq mi (3051 km²) 706 sq mi (1829 km²), 37.46%
Population - (2000) - Density	8903 8/sq mi (3/km²)
Website	www.schoolcraftcounty.net [2]

Schoolcraft County is a county in the Upper Peninsula of the state of Michigan. As of the 2000 census, the population was 8,903. The county seat is Manistique, which lies along the northern shore of Lake Michigan. The county is named in honor of Henry Schoolcraft, who explored the area with the expedition of Lewis Cass. The county is largely rural and forested, with much of western portion of the county located within Hiawatha National Forest.

Geography

According to the U.S. Census Bureau, the county has a total area of 1,884 square miles (4,879 km²), of which, 1,178 square miles (3,051 km²) of it is land and 706 square miles (1,827 km²) of it (37.46%) is water.

Transportation

US Highways

- US 2

Michigan State Trunklines

- M-28
- M-77
- M-94
- M-149

Schoolcraft County Intercounty Highways

- H-13
- H-42
- H-44
- H-52

Federal Forest Highways

- Federal Forest Highway 13 (FFH-13)

Adjacent counties

- Luce County (northeast)
- Mackinac County (southeast)
- Delta County (southwest)
- Alger County (northwest)

National protected areas

- Hiawatha National Forest (part)
- Seney National Wildlife Refuge

Demographics

Rural road in Schoolcraft County

As of the census of 2000, there were 8,903 people, 3,606 households, and 2,498 families residing in the county. The population density was 8 people per square mile (3/km²). There were 5,700 housing units at an average density of 5 per square mile (2/km²). The racial makeup of the county was 88.67% White, 1.63% Black or African American, 6.12% Native American, 0.42% Asian, 0.37% from other races, and 2.80% from two or more races. 0.93% of the population were Hispanic or Latino of any race. 18.6% were of German, 11.0% French, 8.7% Swedish, 8.1% English, 7.4% French Canadian, 6.7% United States or American and 6.4% Irish ancestry according to Census 2000. 98.1% spoke English as their first language.

There were 3,606 households out of which 28.10% had children under the age of 18 living with them, 57.60% were married couples living together, 8.10% had a female householder with no husband present, and 30.70% were non-families. 27.40% of all households were made up of individuals and 13.00% had someone living alone who was 65 years of age or older. The average household size was 2.36 and the average family size was 2.84.

In the county the population was spread out with 22.80% under the age of 18, 6.80% from 18 to 24, 26.10% from 25 to 44, 25.80% from 45 to 64, and 18.60% who were 65 years of age or older. The median age was 41 years. For every 100 females there were 100.10 males. For every 100 females age 18 and over, there were 99.20 males.

The median income for a household in the county was $31,140, and the median income for a family was $36,810. Males had a median income of $32,725 versus $21,364 for females. The per capita income for the county was $17,137. About 9.10% of families and 12.20% of the population were below the poverty line, including 15.40% of those under age 18 and 7.60% of those age 65 or over.

Government

Schoolcraft County operates the County jail, Schoolcraft County Public Transit, maintains rural roads, operates the major local courts, keeps files of deeds and mortgages, maintains vital records, administers public health regulations, and participates with the state in the provision of welfare and other social services. The county board of commissioners controls the budget but has only limited authority to make laws or ordinances. In Michigan, most local government functions — police and fire, building and zoning, tax assessment, street maintenance, etc. — are the responsibility of individual cities and townships.

Schoolcraft County elected officials

- Prosecuting Attorney: Peter J. Hollenbeck
- Sheriff: Grant S. Harris Undersheriff Michael Gierke
- County Clerk/Register of Deeds: Daniel R. McKinney
- County Treasurer: Terri A. Evonich
- Drain Commissioner: Paul Hoholik
- County Surveyor: Thomas P. O'Brien
- Road Commissioners: Gregory Hase; Thomas Klarich; Bernard Lund

(information as of September 2005)

Cities, villages, and townships

- Doyle Township
- Germfask Township
- Hiawatha Township
- Inwood Township
- Manistique Township
- Manistique, city
- Mueller Township
- Seney Township
- Thompson Township

Registered historic places

List of Registered Historic Places in Schoolcraft County:

- Ten Curves Road-Manistique River Bridge — Ten Curves Rd. over Manistique River in Gemfask Township (added 1999-12-17)
- Manistique East Breakwater Light — at offshore end of east breakwater, approx. 1,800 ft. from shore in Manistique (added 2005-09-06
- Manistique Pumping Station — Deer St. in Manistique (added 1981-10-26)
- Seul Choix Pointe Light Station — County Rd. 431 in Manistique (added 1984-07-19)
- Ekdahl-Goudreau Site — address restricted (added 1978-11-16)

Source: National Register Information System [3]

External links

- Schoolcraft County [4]

Geographical coordinates: 46°01′N 86°11′W

Attractions

Tahquamenon Falls

The Upper Tahquamenon Falls

Location	Tahquamenon Falls State Park, Luce County, Michigan
Coordinates	46°34′26″N 85°15′22″W
Type	Block
Total height	48 ft
Number of drops	6
Average flow rate	7,000 gallons per second (average annual mean) Data courtesy USGS [1]
Watercourse	Tahquamenon River

The **Tahquamenon Falls** are two different waterfalls on the Tahquamenon River. Both sets are located near Lake Superior in the eastern Upper Peninsula of Michigan. The water is notably brown in color from the tannins leached from the cedar swamps which the river drains. This phenomenon is responsible for the alternative local name 'Root Beer Falls'.

The upper falls are more than 200 feet (60 m) across and with a drop of approximately 48 feet (14 m) During the late spring runoff, the river drains as much as 50,000 gallons (200,000 liters) of water per second, making the upper falls the third most voluminous vertical waterfall east of the Mississippi River, after Niagara Falls and Cohoes Falls, both in New York State.

The Lower Falls

The lower falls, located four miles (6.5 km) downstream, are a series of five smaller falls cascading around an island which can be reached by rowboat. A hiking trail runs between the falls along the riverside, and visitors often play in the lower falls during the summer heat.

The falls are within the Tahquamenon Falls State Park, between Newberry, Michigan, and Paradise, Michigan. They are a popular tourist destination in the Upper Peninsula during all seasons. Snowmobile trails lead almost to the falls, and walkways are kept clear for most of the winter.

The Tahquamenon is noted as being the land of Longfellow's *The Song of Hiawatha* - "by the rushing Tahquamenaw" where Hiawatha built his canoe. "Tahquamenon Falls" is also a song from Sufjan Stevens's album *Michigan*.

While the name Tahquamenon is now primarily associated with the falls, it appears to have originally designated an island in Whitefish Bay: Tahquamenon Island. The first written record of the name appears as "Outakouaminan" in a 1671 French map.[2]

The upper falls are located at 46°34′29″N 85°15′23″W and the lower falls are at 46°36′12″N 85°12′25″W

Photo gallery

Upper Falls in Winter 2004

During Autumn

The Upper Falls

Panoramic view of Upper Tahquamenon falls in early spring season

External links

- Tahquamenon Falls State Park [3]
- Superior Sights entry on Tahquamenon Falls [4]
- 1961 Life Magazine Photo [5]

Tahquamenon Falls State Park

Tahquamenon Falls State Park	
IUCN Category V (Protected Landscape/Seascape)	
Location	Chippewa / Luce counties, Michigan, USA
Nearest city	Paradise, Michigan
Coordinates	46°33′24″N 85°9′55″W
Area	46,179 acres (186.9 km²)
Visitors	500,000(in)
Governing body	Michigan Department of Natural Resources

The **Tahquamenon Falls State Park** is a 46,179-acre (186.9 km²) state park in the U.S. state of Michigan. It is the second largest of Michigan's state parks. Bordering on Lake Superior, most of the park is located within Chippewa County, with the western section of the park extending into Luce County. The nearest town of any size is Paradise.

Tahquamenon Falls State Park

Tahquamenon Falls is the centerpiece of the park (upper falls pictured).

Tahquamenon Falls State Park follows the Tahquamenon River as it passes over Tahquamenon Falls and drains into Whitefish Bay, Lake Superior. The Tahquamenon Falls include a single 50-foot (15-meter) drop, the *Upper Falls*, plus the cascades and rapids collectively called the *Lower Falls*. During the late-spring runoff, the river drains as much as 50,000 gallons (200,000 liters) of water per second, making the upper falls the second most voluminous vertical waterfall east of the Mississippi River, after only Niagara Falls.

The North Country Trail passes through the park. There is a seasonal shuttle service that allows hikers to walk between upper falls and lower falls without doubling back.

Tahquamenon Falls is also called "Rootbeer Falls" because of its golden-brown color, caused by tannins from cedar swamps that drain into the river. In winter, the ice that accumulates around and in the falls is often colored in shades of green and blue.

Much of the park is undeveloped but it does have more than 22 miles (35 km) of hiking trails. Row boats and canoes are rented to use to approach the lower falls. There are five campgrounds in the park with a total of 350 campsites. The park receives as many as 500,000 visitors per year, many of whom drive in on the state park's only paved road, M-123. M-123 intersects with Interstate 75 at Michigan exit #352.

Nearby attractions include the Great Lakes Shipwreck Museum at Whitefish Point, and the Point Iroquois Light and Museum at Bay Mills, Michigan on Whitefish Bay.

External links

- Tahquamenon Falls State Park [1], official website
- Tahquamenon Falls State Park [2]
- World Database on Protected Areas - Tahquamenon Falls State Park [3]

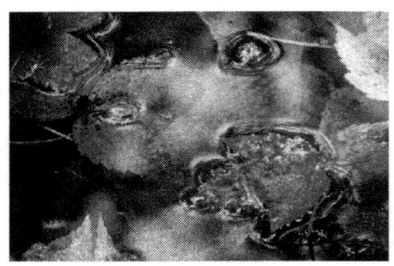

Fall colors on a rainy day, 1991

Tahquamenon River

The **Tahquamenon River** is a 94-mile (151 km) long blackwater river in the U.S. state of Michigan that flows in a generally eastward direction through the eastern end of the Upper Peninsula. It drains approximately 820 square miles (2120 km^2) of the Upper Peninsula, including large sections of Luce County and Chippewa County. It begins in the Tahquamenon Lakes in northeast Columbus Township of Luce County and empties into Lake Superior near the village of Paradise. M-123 runs alongside a portion of the river.

The Upper Falls on the Tahquamenon River.

Name

The meaning of "Tahquamenon" is not known. Some called it the "River of the Head Winds" because they bucked the wind on the lower river no matter what direction they were paddling. Others called it the "River of a Hundred Bends". Twentieth century descendants of local Chippewa translated the name to mean "river up against a hill" or "lost river island" or "river with an island part way". In 1930 Jesuit scholar, Father William Gagnieut, concluded that the meaning of the name had been lost.

Recorded variously as 'Otikwaminang,' 'Outakwamenon,' 'Tequamenen', 'Tanguamanon,' 'Tanquamanon,' 'Toumequellen' and 'Tahquamenaw', several suggestions on the meaning of its name have been made over the years:

- The origin of the present spelling can be traced to a Jesuit map of Lake Superior published in 1672 that named the small island lying 5 miles (8.0 km) off the river mouth as "Outa koua minan'. The early French travelers called the Great Lakes region natives "Outaouaks".
- "Marsh of the blueberries," though 'menon' (*miinan*) does mean "blueberries" in the Ojibwa language, 'tahqua' does not mean "marsh"
- "Short cornel" where 'tahqua' (*dakwaa*) does mean "short" and 'manan' (*maanan*) does mean "cornel", but cornels do not grow in swamplands
- "Ottawa's good land" (*Odaawaag minaang*) due to an Ottawa village that used to be located near the mouth of the river

The current name for the Tahquamenon River in the Ojibwa language is *Adikamegong-ziibi* "River at where the Whitefish are found." This name is also the naming basis for the Whitefish Point and

Whitefish Bay, both known earlier as "Tahquamenaw".

Tahquamenon Falls

The river is best known for the Tahquamenon Falls, a succession of two waterfalls in Tahquamenon Falls State Park totalling approximately 73 feet (22 m) in height. Because the headwaters of the river are located in a boreal wetland that is rich in cedar, spruce and hemlock trees, the river's waters carry a significant amount of tannin in solution (i.e., it is a blackwater river), and are often brown or golden-brown in color. The Tahquamenon Falls are thus acclaimed as being the largest naturally dyed or colored waterfall in the United States. The state park preserves the falls area and some 24 miles (39 km) of the river.

Recreation

In Henry Wadsworth Longfellow's once-famous poem, *The Song of Hiawatha* (1855), the hero learned how to paddle a birchbark canoe in the Tahquamenon. The river is often used for canoeing to this day. The river's watershed and state park are also extensively used for fishing and hiking. In winter, the watershed welcomes snowmobilers.

Tour boat

The *Toonerville Trolley Train and Riverboat Tour*, a private firm, offers 21-mile (34 km) boat tours of the upper Tahquamenon as part of an overall family experience that includes a narrow-gauge rail ride and visit to the Upper Tahquamenon Falls. The tour is based in Soo Junction, between Newberry and Hulbert.

References

- Taylor, Sprague, (1991, 2008). *Tahquamenon Country: A look at the past*. Historical Society of Michigan, East Lansing, Michigan. ISBN 978-0-87013833-1.

External links

- Tahquamenon Falls State Park [2]
- Toonerville Trolley Riverboat Tour [1]

Muskallonge Lake State Park

Muskallonge Lake State Park is a state park in Michigan. It is located 28 miles (45 km) northwest of Newberry in Luce County. The 217-acre (0.88 km^2) park is situated between the shores of Lake Superior and Muskallonge Lake and the area is well known for its forests, lakes and streams. Muskallonge Lake State Park was the former site of Deer Park, a lumbering town in the late 1880s, and prior to its lumbering history, an Indian encampment. Muskallonge Lake was a mill pond for millions of white pine logs that were brought to it by railroad lines. By 1900, the virgin stands of pines were depleted, the mill was closed, and the lumbering operation moved away. All that remains as evidence of the lumbering community are piles of sawdust and a few partly submerged pine logs in the lake.

Deer Park (formerly Muskallong Lake) Station was one of five U.S. Life-Saving Service Stations along the coast of Lake Superior between Munising and Whitefish Point in the Upper Peninsula of Michigan. It was part of the U.S. Life-Saving Service District 10 (later part of District 11). The other four Life-saving Stations were Grand Marais, Two Heart, Crisp Point Light, and Vermilion Point. In 1915, these stations became part of the U.S. Coast Guard. In 1939 the U.S. Lighthouse Service also merged under the control of the U.S. Coast Guard.

See also

List of lifesaving stations in Michigan

External links

- Department of Natural Resources [1]
- U.S. Coast Guard Search & Rescue Index [2]

USCG Station Deer Park [3]

Geographical coordinates: 46°39′45″N 85°39′18″W

Transportation

Sault Ste. Marie Airport

Sault Ste. Marie Airport	

IATA: YAM – ICAO: CYAM	
Summary	
Airport type	Public
Operator	Sault Ste. Marie Airport Development Corporation
Location	Sault Ste. Marie, Ontario
Hub for	{{{hub}}}
Elevation AMSL	630 ft / 192 m
Coordinates	46°29′06″N 084°30′35″W
Website	www.SaultAirport.com [1]

Runways			
Direction	Length		Surface
	ft	m	
04/22	5,990	1826	Asphalt
12/30	5,991	1826	Asphalt

Statistics (2009)	
Aircraft Movements	50,987
Sources: Canada Flight Supplement Movements from Statistics Canada	

Sault Ste. Marie Airport, (IATA: **YAM**, ICAO: **CYAM**), is an international airport located 8.0 NM (14.8 km; 9.2 mi) west-southwest of the city of Sault Ste. Marie, Ontario, Canada at the far eastern end of Lake Superior and the beginning of the St. Mary's River.

History

The Canadian government opened the airport in 1961 and operated it until 1998, when it handed control over to the newly-formed Sault Ste. Marie Airport Development Corporation (SSMADC) under the terms of the National Airports Policy. Of the 23 Ontario regional, local, or small airports handed over under the policy, the Sault Ste. Marie airport is the only one not affiliated with a municipality, since the city of Sault Ste. Marie declined to assume control. In 2002, the SSMADC opened *Runway Park*, an entertainment and recreation area, on unused airport property to help generate revenue to support the airport's operation.

Airlines and destinations

Airlines	Destinations
Air Canada Jazz	Toronto-Pearson
Bearskin Airlines	North Bay, Ottawa, Sudbury, Thunder Bay
Sunwing Airlines	Cancun, Varadero (seasonal)

Operations

The Sault Ste. Marie airport has equipment to support instrument approaches for all-weather operation, as well as a NavCanada control tower and onsite flight service station. Its runways are designed to handle medium-sized transport jets such as the Airbus A320 and Boeing 737, current operations to Sault Ste. Marie consist of turboprop and Boeing 737 aircraft.

In 2009, the airport ranked 34th among Canadian airports for total number of aircraft movements (landing or taking off), with 50,987 movements. Of those, 25,306 were by itinerant aircraft, and 25,6815 were local movements.

The airport is classifed as an airport of entry by NAV CANADA and is staffed by the Canada Border Services Agency. CBSA officers at this airport currently can handle aircraft with no more than 30 passengers.

General aviation operations

The airport hosts the flight-training campus for Sault College as well as the *Soo Aviation* flying school, resulting in frequent training flights in the vicinity. It is also the site of the Ministry of Natural Resources Fire Management Centre. In addition to these, the Sault Ste. Marie airport has frequent medevac, business aviation, and charter operations. It is a frequent stopping point for private pilots.

See also

- Sault Ste. Marie Water Aerodrome
- Sault Ste. Marie/Partridge Point Water Aerodrome

External links

- Sault Ste. Marie Airport [1] (official site)
- Sault College Aviation Technology [2]
- Soo Aviation [3]
- Runway Park [4]
- Accident history for YAM [5] at Aviation Safety Network
- Past three hours METARs, SPECI and current TAFs for Sault Ste. Marie Airport [6] from NAV CANADA as available.

Article Sources and Contributors

Luce County, Michigan *Source*: http://en.wikipedia.org/?oldid=372960224 *Contributors*:

Michigan *Source*: http://en.wikipedia.org/?oldid=390673209 *Contributors*: JohnInDC

History of Michigan *Source*: http://en.wikipedia.org/?oldid=386013916 *Contributors*: Allmightyduck

Cyrus G. Luce *Source*: http://en.wikipedia.org/?oldid=385638470 *Contributors*:

Upper Peninsula of Michigan *Source*: http://en.wikipedia.org/?oldid=390636931 *Contributors*: 1 anonymous edits

Lake Superior *Source*: http://en.wikipedia.org/?oldid=389341870 *Contributors*: Abutorsam007

Newberry, Michigan *Source*: http://en.wikipedia.org/?oldid=389337579 *Contributors*: 1 anonymous edits

Columbus Township, Luce County, Michigan *Source*: http://en.wikipedia.org/?oldid=333143804 *Contributors*: Dabomb87

Lakefield Township, Luce County, Michigan *Source*: http://en.wikipedia.org/?oldid=383296777 *Contributors*:

McMillan Township, Luce County, Michigan *Source*: http://en.wikipedia.org/?oldid=383296964 *Contributors*: Dabomb87

Pentland Township, Michigan *Source*: http://en.wikipedia.org/?oldid=368845518 *Contributors*:

Alger County, Michigan *Source*: http://en.wikipedia.org/?oldid=383059755 *Contributors*: Omnedon

Chippewa County, Michigan *Source*: http://en.wikipedia.org/?oldid=385270199 *Contributors*: Omnedon

Mackinac County, Michigan *Source*: http://en.wikipedia.org/?oldid=387249239 *Contributors*: Parkerdr

Schoolcraft County, Michigan *Source*: http://en.wikipedia.org/?oldid=375164071 *Contributors*:

Tahquamenon Falls *Source*: http://en.wikipedia.org/?oldid=360750114 *Contributors*: Bkonrad

Tahquamenon Falls State Park *Source*: http://en.wikipedia.org/?oldid=378807584 *Contributors*: Tfunke

Tahquamenon River *Source*: http://en.wikipedia.org/?oldid=378137428 *Contributors*: Aristophanes68

Muskallonge Lake State Park *Source*: http://en.wikipedia.org/?oldid=354290343 *Contributors*:

Sault Ste. Marie Airport *Source*: http://en.wikipedia.org/?oldid=382915415 *Contributors*: CambridgeBayWeather

Image Sources, Licenses and Contributors

File:Map of Michigan highlighting Luce County.svg *Source*: http://bibliocm.bibliolabs.com/mwAnon/index.php?title=File:Map_of_Michigan_highlighting_Luce_County.svg *License*: Public Domain *Contributors*: User:Dbenbenn

File:Map of USA MI.svg *Source*: http://bibliocm.bibliolabs.com/mwAnon/index.php?title=File:Map_of_USA_MI.svg *License*: Creative Commons Attribution 2.0 *Contributors*: Abnormaal, Hogweard, Huebi, Lokal Profil, Lupo, Mattbuck, Petr Dlouhý, 2 anonymous edits

File:2009-0618-Newberry-LuceCtyBuilding.jpg *Source*: http://bibliocm.bibliolabs.com/mwAnon/index.php?title=File:2009-0618-Newberry-LuceCtyBuilding.jpg *License*: Creative Commons Attribution 2.5 *Contributors*: Bobak Ha'Eri

Image:M-28.svg *Source*: http://bibliocm.bibliolabs.com/mwAnon/index.php?title=File:M-28.svg *License*: Public Domain *Contributors*: User:IW4

Image:M-117.svg *Source*: http://bibliocm.bibliolabs.com/mwAnon/index.php?title=File:M-117.svg *License*: Public Domain *Contributors*: User:IW4

Image:M-123.svg *Source*: http://bibliocm.bibliolabs.com/mwAnon/index.php?title=File:M-123.svg *License*: Public Domain *Contributors*: User:IW4

Image:Michigan H-33 Luce County.svg *Source*: http://bibliocm.bibliolabs.com/mwAnon/index.php?title=File:Michigan_H-33_Luce_County.svg *License*: Public Domain *Contributors*: User:IW4

Image:Michigan H-37 Luce County.svg *Source*: http://bibliocm.bibliolabs.com/mwAnon/index.php?title=File:Michigan_H-37_Luce_County.svg *License*: Public Domain *Contributors*: User:IW4

Image:Michigan H-44 Schoolcraft County.svg *Source*: http://bibliocm.bibliolabs.com/mwAnon/index.php?title=File:Michigan_H-44_Schoolcraft_County.svg *License*: Public Domain *Contributors*: User:IW4

Image:Michigan H-58 Luce County.svg *Source*: http://bibliocm.bibliolabs.com/mwAnon/index.php?title=File:Michigan_H-58_Luce_County.svg *License*: Public Domain *Contributors*: User:IW4

File:Flag_of_Michigan.svg *Source*: http://bibliocm.bibliolabs.com/mwAnon/index.php?title=File:Flag_of_Michigan.svg *License*: unknown *Contributors*: Awg1010, Denelson83, Dzordzm, Fry1989, Homo lupus, Mattes, Serinde, Svgalbertian, Werewombat, 1 anonymous edits

File:Seal of Michigan.svg *Source*: http://bibliocm.bibliolabs.com/mwAnon/index.php?title=File:Seal_of_Michigan.svg *License*: unknown *Contributors*: Designed by Lewis Cass

File:Map_of_USA_MI.svg *Source*: http://bibliocm.bibliolabs.com/mwAnon/index.php?title=File:Map_of_USA_MI.svg *License*: Creative Commons Attribution 2.0 *Contributors*: Abnormaal, Hogweard, Huebi, Lokal Profil, Lupo, Mattbuck, Petr Dlouhý, 2 anonymous edits

File:Michigan 1718.jpg *Source*: http://bibliocm.bibliolabs.com/mwAnon/index.php?title=File:Michigan_1718.jpg *License*: Public Domain *Contributors*: Original uploader was Billwhittaker at en.wikipedia

File:Hauling at Thomas Foster's, by Jenney, J A (detail).jpg *Source*: http://bibliocm.bibliolabs.com/mwAnon/index.php?title=File:Hauling_at_Thomas_Foster's,_by_Jenney,_J_A_(detail).jpg *License*: Public Domain *Contributors*: Rmhermen

File:Granholm speaking to troops, Lansing, 1 Dec, 2005.jpg *Source*: http://bibliocm.bibliolabs.com/mwAnon/index.php?title=File:Granholm_speaking_to_troops,_Lansing,_1_Dec,_2005.jpg *License*: Public Domain *Contributors*: SFC Jim Dowen, Jr.

File:Sleeping Bear Dune Aerial View.jpg *Source*: http://bibliocm.bibliolabs.com/mwAnon/index.php?title=File:Sleeping_Bear_Dune_Aerial_View.jpg *License*: Public Domain *Contributors*: National Park Service employee

File:Tahquamenon falls upper.jpg *Source*: http://bibliocm.bibliolabs.com/mwAnon/index.php?title=File:Tahquamenon_falls_upper.jpg *License*: Creative Commons Attribution 2.5 *Contributors*: User:anagy

File:Pointe Mouillee.jpg *Source*: http://bibliocm.bibliolabs.com/mwAnon/index.php?title=File:Pointe_Mouillee.jpg *License*: Public Domain *Contributors*: U.S. Army Corps of Engineers, photographer not specified or unknown

File:Little Sable Light Point Light Station - Michigan.jpg *Source*: http://bibliocm.bibliolabs.com/mwAnon/index.php?title=File:Little_Sable_Light_Point_Light_Station_-_Michigan.jpg *License*: Creative Commons Attribution 2.5 *Contributors*: Jjegers at en.wikipedia

File:Michigan.svg *Source*: http://bibliocm.bibliolabs.com/mwAnon/index.php?title=File:Michigan.svg *License*: GNU Free Documentation License *Contributors*: Phizzy (talk).

File:MichiganHardinessZones.svg *Source*: http://bibliocm.bibliolabs.com/mwAnon/index.php?title=File:MichiganHardinessZones.svg *License*: GNU Free Documentation License *Contributors*: Phizzy (talk).

File:Michigan population map.png *Source*: http://bibliocm.bibliolabs.com/mwAnon/index.php?title=File:Michigan_population_map.png *License*: GNU Free Documentation License *Contributors*: Original uploader was JimIrwin at en.wikipedia

File:MichiganAncestry.svg *Source*: http://bibliocm.bibliolabs.com/mwAnon/index.php?title=File:MichiganAncestry.svg *License*: GNU Free Documentation License *Contributors*: Phizzy (talk). Original uploader was Phizzy at en.wikipedia

File:Michigan Cherries, 2009 July.jpg *Source*: http://bibliocm.bibliolabs.com/mwAnon/index.php?title=File:Michigan_Cherries,_2009_July.jpg *License*: Creative Commons Attribution 2.0 *Contributors*: Steven Depolo

File:Grand Hotel-Mackinac Island.jpg *Source*: http://bibliocm.bibliolabs.com/mwAnon/index.php?title=File:Grand_Hotel-Mackinac_Island.jpg *License*: Attribution *Contributors*: David Ball

File:Mackinac Bridge Sunset.jpg *Source*: http://bibliocm.bibliolabs.com/mwAnon/index.php?title=File:Mackinac_Bridge_Sunset.jpg *License*: Creative Commons Attribution 3.0 *Contributors*: User:Dehk

File:Michigan entrance sign.JPG *Source*: http://bibliocm.bibliolabs.com/mwAnon/index.php?title=File:Michigan_entrance_sign.JPG *License*: Public Domain *Contributors*: User:Lovemykia

File:Grskyline2.jpg *Source*: http://bibliocm.bibliolabs.com/mwAnon/index.php?title=File:Grskyline2.jpg *License*: Public Domain *Contributors*: User:Bhyse23

File:1 Lansing Pan.jpg *Source*: http://bibliocm.bibliolabs.com/mwAnon/index.php?title=File:1_Lansing_Pan.jpg *License*: GNU Free Documentation License *Contributors*: User Criticalthinker on en.wikipedia

Image Sources, Licenses and Contributors

File:Flint skyline2.jpg *Source*: http://bibliocm.bibliolabs.com/mwAnon/index.php?title=File:Flint_skyline2.jpg *License*: Public Domain *Contributors*: Xnatedawgx, Yassie

File:DownTownAA1 copy.jpg *Source*: http://bibliocm.bibliolabs.com/mwAnon/index.php?title=File:DownTownAA1_copy.jpg *License*: Creative Commons Attribution 3.0 *Contributors*: Alan Piracha (Alanmi88)

File:MichiganCities.svg *Source*: http://bibliocm.bibliolabs.com/mwAnon/index.php?title=File:MichiganCities.svg *License*: GNU Free Documentation License *Contributors*: Phizzy (talk).

File:Flag of Japan.svg *Source*: http://bibliocm.bibliolabs.com/mwAnon/index.php?title=File:Flag_of_Japan.svg *License*: Public Domain *Contributors*: Various

File:Flag of the People's Republic of China.svg *Source*: http://bibliocm.bibliolabs.com/mwAnon/index.php?title=File:Flag_of_the_People's_Republic_of_China.svg *License*: Public Domain *Contributors*: User:Denelson83, User:SKopp, User:Shizhao, User:Zscout370

Image:Soo Locks-Sault-Ste Marie.png *Source*: http://bibliocm.bibliolabs.com/mwAnon/index.php?title=File:Soo_Locks-Sault-Ste_Marie.png *License*: Public Domain *Contributors*: AnRo0002, Appraiser, Feydey, Geofrog, Jkelly, Juiced lemon, Kimdime, Mattes, Mircea, Rmhermen, Skeezix1000, Xnatedawgx, Yassie, 5 anonymous edits

Image:Last glacial vegetation map.png *Source*: http://bibliocm.bibliolabs.com/mwAnon/index.php?title=File:Last_glacial_vegetation_map.png *License*: unknown *Contributors*: Ciaurlec, DieBuche, Fabartus, Glenn, Innotata, JMCC1, Joey-das-WBF, Jrockley, MaxEnt, Mmcannis, Santosga, SchumirWeb, Slomox, 4 anonymous edits

Image:Michigan 1718.jpg *Source*: http://bibliocm.bibliolabs.com/mwAnon/index.php?title=File:Michigan_1718.jpg *License*: Public Domain *Contributors*: Original uploader was Billwhittaker at en.wikipedia

Image:Treaty of Paris by Benjamin West 1783.jpg *Source*: http://bibliocm.bibliolabs.com/mwAnon/index.php?title=File:Treaty_of_Paris_by_Benjamin_West_1783.jpg *License*: Public Domain *Contributors*: Bogdan, Clindberg, Daderot, Jkllee, Man vyi, Nonenmac, Shakko, The Red Hat of Pat Ferrick

Image:Flint Sit-Down Strike window.jpg *Source*: http://bibliocm.bibliolabs.com/mwAnon/index.php?title=File:Flint_Sit-Down_Strike_window.jpg *License*: unknown *Contributors*: Sheldon Dick

Image:Gerald Ford.jpg *Source*: http://bibliocm.bibliolabs.com/mwAnon/index.php?title=File:Gerald_Ford.jpg *License*: Public Domain *Contributors*: David Hume Kennerly, White House.

Image:Porcupine Mountains Michigan.jpg *Source*: http://bibliocm.bibliolabs.com/mwAnon/index.php?title=File:Porcupine_Mountains_Michigan.jpg *License*: Creative Commons Attribution 2.0 *Contributors*: w:Flickr user Erik Abderhalden

File:Flag of the United States.svg *Source*: http://bibliocm.bibliolabs.com/mwAnon/index.php?title=File:Flag_of_the_United_States.svg *License*: Public Domain *Contributors*: User:Dbenbenn, User:Indolences, User:Jacobolus, User:Technion, User:Zscout370

File:Flag of Michigan.svg *Source*: http://bibliocm.bibliolabs.com/mwAnon/index.php?title=File:Flag_of_Michigan.svg *License*: unknown *Contributors*: Awg1010, Denelson83, Dzordzm, Fry1989, Homo lupus, Mattes, Serinde, Svgalbertian, Werewombat, 1 anonymous edits

Image:MichiganUpperPeninsula.svg *Source*: http://bibliocm.bibliolabs.com/mwAnon/index.php?title=File:MichiganUpperPeninsula.svg *License*: GNU Free Documentation License *Contributors*: Phizzy (talk).

File:Pictured Rocks Lakeshore Michigan3.JPG *Source*: http://bibliocm.bibliolabs.com/mwAnon/index.php?title=File:Pictured_Rocks_Lakeshore_Michigan3.JPG *License*: unknown *Contributors*: MJCdetroit

File:Cabin on Blue Lake in UP.jpg *Source*: http://bibliocm.bibliolabs.com/mwAnon/index.php?title=File:Cabin_on_Blue_Lake_in_UP.jpg *License*: Creative Commons Attribution-Sharealike 3.0 *Contributors*: User:MJCdetroit

File:Central Mine Historic District MI 2009 Powderhouse.jpg *Source*: http://bibliocm.bibliolabs.com/mwAnon/index.php?title=File:Central_Mine_Historic_District_MI_2009_Powderhouse.jpg *License*: Creative Commons Attribution-Sharealike 3.0 *Contributors*: User:Andrew Jameson

File:Mackinac-Bridge-Snowstorm-February-20-2006.jpg *Source*: http://bibliocm.bibliolabs.com/mwAnon/index.php?title=File:Mackinac-Bridge-Snowstorm-February-20-2006.jpg *License*: Creative Commons Attribution 2.5 *Contributors*: BLueFiSH.as, Fran Rogers, Mrmiscellanious, Parkerdr, Werewombat, Xnatedawgx

File:I-75.svg *Source*: http://bibliocm.bibliolabs.com/mwAnon/index.php?title=File:I-75.svg *License*: unknown *Contributors*: Augiasstallputzer, Ltljltlj, SPUI, 1 anonymous edits

File:US 2.svg *Source*: http://bibliocm.bibliolabs.com/mwAnon/index.php?title=File:US_2.svg *License*: Public Domain *Contributors*: SPUI, 1 anonymous edits

File:US 41.svg *Source*: http://bibliocm.bibliolabs.com/mwAnon/index.php?title=File:US_41.svg *License*: Public Domain *Contributors*: Rocket000, SPUI

File:US 45.svg *Source*: http://bibliocm.bibliolabs.com/mwAnon/index.php?title=File:US_45.svg *License*: Public Domain *Contributors*: Luigi Chiesa, SPUI, Xnatedawgx

File:US 141.svg *Source*: http://bibliocm.bibliolabs.com/mwAnon/index.php?title=File:US_141.svg *License*: Public Domain *Contributors*: SPUI

File:M-28.svg *Source*: http://bibliocm.bibliolabs.com/mwAnon/index.php?title=File:M-28.svg *License*: Public Domain *Contributors*: User:IW4

File:2009-0617-DaYooperTouristTrap.jpg *Source*: http://bibliocm.bibliolabs.com/mwAnon/index.php?title=File:2009-0617-DaYooperTouristTrap.jpg *License*: Creative Commons Attribution 2.5 *Contributors*: Bobak Ha'Eri

File:2009-0618-PASTIES-w00t.JPG *Source*: http://bibliocm.bibliolabs.com/mwAnon/index.php?title=File:2009-0618-PASTIES-w00t.JPG *License*: Creative Commons Attribution 2.5 *Contributors*: Bobak Ha'Eri

file:Lake Superior NASA.jpg *Source*: http://bibliocm.bibliolabs.com/mwAnon/index.php?title=File:Lake_Superior_NASA.jpg *License*: Public Domain *Contributors*: Mircea, Svenskan

file:Lake-Superior.svg *Source*: http://bibliocm.bibliolabs.com/mwAnon/index.php?title=File:Lake-Superior.svg *License*: GNU Free Documentation License *Contributors*: Phizzy (talk). Original uploader was Phizzy at en.wikipedia

File:LakeSuperior from Duluth in Winter.jpg *Source*: http://bibliocm.bibliolabs.com/mwAnon/index.php?title=File:LakeSuperior_from_Duluth_in_Winter.jpg *License*: Creative Commons Attribution-Sharealike 2.5 *Contributors*: Magog the Ogre, Yassie

Image:Superior amo 2009062 lrg.jpg *Source*: http://bibliocm.bibliolabs.com/mwAnon/index.php?title=File:Superior_amo_2009062_lrg.jpg *License*: Public Domain *Contributors*: NASA image courtesy MODIS Rapid Response Team, Goddard Space Flight Center. Caption by Michon Scott based on image interpretation by Walt Meier, National Snow and Ice Data Center.

File:Geologic Map Lake Superior MN WI MI.jpg *Source*: http://bibliocm.bibliolabs.com/mwAnon/index.php?title=File:Geologic_Map_Lake_Superior_MN_WI_MI.jpg *License*: unknown *Contributors*: Morey, G. B., Sims, P. K. Cannon, W. F., Mudrey, M. G., Jr., D. L. Southwick

Image:North america basement rocks.png *Source*: http://bibliocm.bibliolabs.com/mwAnon/index.php?title=File:North_america_basement_rocks.png *License*: unknown *Contributors*: User:SEWilco

Image Sources, Licenses and Contributors

Image:AgawaRock23.jpg *Source*: http://bibliocm.bibliolabs.com/mwAnon/index.php?title=File:AgawaRock23.jpg *License*: Creative Commons Attribution-Sharealike 2.0 *Contributors*: Big iron, Lord Hidelan, P199, RedWolf, Wsiegmund

Image:050820 GrandPortageNationalMonument.jpg *Source*: http://bibliocm.bibliolabs.com/mwAnon/index.php?title=File:050820_GrandPortageNationalMonument.jpg *License*: unknown *Contributors*: Rufus Sarsaparilla on wikipédia en

Image:Lake Superior at Neys Provincial Park Ontario.jpg *Source*: http://bibliocm.bibliolabs.com/mwAnon/index.php?title=File:Lake_Superior_at_Neys_Provincial_Park_Ontario.jpg *License*: Creative Commons Attribution-Sharealike 3.0 *Contributors*: User:Kevstan

Image:Miners Castle, Pictured Rocks National Lakeshore.jpg *Source*: http://bibliocm.bibliolabs.com/mwAnon/index.php?title=File:Miners_Castle,_Pictured_Rocks_National_Lakeshore.jpg *License*: Creative Commons Attribution 2.0 *Contributors*: User:Daniel Case

File:Luce_County_Michigan_Incorporated_and_Unincorporated_areas_Newberry_Highlighted.svg *Source*: http://bibliocm.bibliolabs.com/mwAnon/index.php?title=File:Luce_County_Michigan_Incorporated_and_Unincorporated_areas_Newberry_Highlighted.svg *License*: Creative Commons Attribution-Sharealike 2.5 *Contributors*: Arkyan

File:2009-0618-Newberry-LuceCtyMuseum.jpg *Source*: http://bibliocm.bibliolabs.com/mwAnon/index.php?title=File:2009-0618-Newberry-LuceCtyMuseum.jpg *License*: Creative Commons Attribution 2.5 *Contributors*: Bobak Ha'Eri

File:2009-0618-Newberry-McMillanTownship.jpg *Source*: http://bibliocm.bibliolabs.com/mwAnon/index.php?title=File:2009-0618-Newberry-McMillanTownship.jpg *License*: Creative Commons Attribution 2.5 *Contributors*: Bobak Ha'Eri

File:USA Michigan location map.svg *Source*: http://bibliocm.bibliolabs.com/mwAnon/index.php?title=File:USA_Michigan_location_map.svg *License*: Creative Commons Attribution 3.0 *Contributors*: User:Alexrk2

File:Red pog.svg *Source*: http://bibliocm.bibliolabs.com/mwAnon/index.php?title=File:Red_pog.svg *License*: Public Domain *Contributors*: User:Andux

File:Map of Michigan highlighting Alger County.svg *Source*: http://bibliocm.bibliolabs.com/mwAnon/index.php?title=File:Map_of_Michigan_highlighting_Alger_County.svg *License*: Public Domain *Contributors*: User:Dbenbenn

File:2009-0618-Munising-AlgerCtyCourt.jpg *Source*: http://bibliocm.bibliolabs.com/mwAnon/index.php?title=File:2009-0618-Munising-AlgerCtyCourt.jpg *License*: Creative Commons Attribution 2.5 *Contributors*: Bobak Ha'Eri

File:M-67.svg *Source*: http://bibliocm.bibliolabs.com/mwAnon/index.php?title=File:M-67.svg *License*: Public Domain *Contributors*: User:IW4

File:M-77.svg *Source*: http://bibliocm.bibliolabs.com/mwAnon/index.php?title=File:M-77.svg *License*: Public Domain *Contributors*: User:IW4

File:M-94.svg *Source*: http://bibliocm.bibliolabs.com/mwAnon/index.php?title=File:M-94.svg *License*: Public Domain *Contributors*: User:IW4

Image:Midway General Store H13 MI.jpg *Source*: http://bibliocm.bibliolabs.com/mwAnon/index.php?title=File:Midway_General_Store_H13_MI.jpg *License*: Creative Commons Attribution-Sharealike 3.0 *Contributors*: User:MJCdetroit

File:Michigan H-01_Alger County.svg *Source*: http://bibliocm.bibliolabs.com/mwAnon/index.php?title=File:Michigan_H-01_Alger_County.svg *License*: Public Domain *Contributors*: User:IW4

File:Michigan H-03_Alger County.svg *Source*: http://bibliocm.bibliolabs.com/mwAnon/index.php?title=File:Michigan_H-03_Alger_County.svg *License*: Public Domain *Contributors*: User:IW4

File:Michigan H-05_Alger County.svg *Source*: http://bibliocm.bibliolabs.com/mwAnon/index.php?title=File:Michigan_H-05_Alger_County.svg *License*: Public Domain *Contributors*: User:IW4

File:Michigan H-11_Alger County.svg *Source*: http://bibliocm.bibliolabs.com/mwAnon/index.php?title=File:Michigan_H-11_Alger_County.svg *License*: Public Domain *Contributors*: User:IW4

File:Michigan H-13_Alger County.svg *Source*: http://bibliocm.bibliolabs.com/mwAnon/index.php?title=File:Michigan_H-13_Alger_County.svg *License*: Public Domain *Contributors*: User:IW4

File:Michigan H-15_Alger County.svg *Source*: http://bibliocm.bibliolabs.com/mwAnon/index.php?title=File:Michigan_H-15_Alger_County.svg *License*: Public Domain *Contributors*: User:Imzadi1979

File:Michigan H-44_Alger County.svg *Source*: http://bibliocm.bibliolabs.com/mwAnon/index.php?title=File:Michigan_H-44_Alger_County.svg *License*: Public Domain *Contributors*: User:IW4

File:Michigan H-52_Alger County.svg *Source*: http://bibliocm.bibliolabs.com/mwAnon/index.php?title=File:Michigan_H-52_Alger_County.svg *License*: Public Domain *Contributors*: User:IW4

File:Michigan H-58_Alger County.svg *Source*: http://bibliocm.bibliolabs.com/mwAnon/index.php?title=File:Michigan_H-58_Alger_County.svg *License*: Public Domain *Contributors*: User:IW4

Image:Forest Route 13.svg *Source*: http://bibliocm.bibliolabs.com/mwAnon/index.php?title=File:Forest_Route_13.svg *License*: unknown *Contributors*: User:Imzadi1979

Image:Pictured Rocks Bridalveil Falls.jpg *Source*: http://bibliocm.bibliolabs.com/mwAnon/index.php?title=File:Pictured_Rocks_Bridalveil_Falls.jpg *License*: Public Domain *Contributors*: National Park Service

File:Map of Michigan highlighting Chippewa County.svg *Source*: http://bibliocm.bibliolabs.com/mwAnon/index.php?title=File:Map_of_Michigan_highlighting_Chippewa_County.svg *License*: Public Domain *Contributors*: User:Dbenbenn

File:2009-0618-Soo-ChippewaCtyCt.jpg *Source*: http://bibliocm.bibliolabs.com/mwAnon/index.php?title=File:2009-0618-Soo-ChippewaCtyCt.jpg *License*: Creative Commons Attribution 2.5 *Contributors*: Bobak Ha'Eri

Image:Chippewa county, MI 1904.png *Source*: http://bibliocm.bibliolabs.com/mwAnon/index.php?title=File:Chippewa_county,_MI_1904.png *License*: Public Domain *Contributors*: Feydey, Juiced lemon, Origamiemensch, Uyvsdi, Werewombat

File:M-48.svg *Source*: http://bibliocm.bibliolabs.com/mwAnon/index.php?title=File:M-48.svg *License*: Public Domain *Contributors*: User:IW4

File:M-80.svg *Source*: http://bibliocm.bibliolabs.com/mwAnon/index.php?title=File:M-80.svg *License*: Public Domain *Contributors*: User:IW4

File:M-123.svg *Source*: http://bibliocm.bibliolabs.com/mwAnon/index.php?title=File:M-123.svg *License*: Public Domain *Contributors*: User:IW4

File:M-129.svg *Source*: http://bibliocm.bibliolabs.com/mwAnon/index.php?title=File:M-129.svg *License*: Public Domain *Contributors*: User:IW4

Image Sources, Licenses and Contributors

File:M-134.svg *Source*: http://bibliocm.bibliolabs.com/mwAnon/index.php?title=File:M-134.svg *License*: Public Domain *Contributors*: User:IW4

File:M-221.svg *Source*: http://bibliocm.bibliolabs.com/mwAnon/index.php?title=File:M-221.svg *License*: Public Domain *Contributors*: User:IW4

File:Business Spur 75.svg *Source*: http://bibliocm.bibliolabs.com/mwAnon/index.php?title=File:Business_Spur_75.svg *License*: unknown *Contributors*: Engleman, I-215, KelleyCook, Ltljltlj, Mountain169257, SPUI, Sehome Bay, T2

File:Michigan H-40_Chippewa County.svg *Source*: http://bibliocm.bibliolabs.com/mwAnon/index.php?title=File:Michigan_H-40_Chippewa_County.svg *License*: Public Domain *Contributors*: User:IW4

File:Michigan H-63_Chippewa County.svg *Source*: http://bibliocm.bibliolabs.com/mwAnon/index.php?title=File:Michigan_H-63_Chippewa_County.svg *License*: Public Domain *Contributors*: User:IW4

File:Map of Michigan highlighting Mackinac County.svg *Source*: http://bibliocm.bibliolabs.com/mwAnon/index.php?title=File:Map_of_Michigan_highlighting_Mackinac_County.svg *License*: Public Domain *Contributors*: User:Dbenbenn

File:Business Loop 75.svg *Source*: http://bibliocm.bibliolabs.com/mwAnon/index.php?title=File:Business_Loop_75.svg *License*: unknown *Contributors*: Engleman, I-215, KelleyCook, Ltljltlj, Mountain169257, SPUI, T2, 1 anonymous edits

File:M-117.svg *Source*: http://bibliocm.bibliolabs.com/mwAnon/index.php?title=File:M-117.svg *License*: Public Domain *Contributors*: User:IW4

Image:M-185 (MISPC).svg *Source*: http://bibliocm.bibliolabs.com/mwAnon/index.php?title=File:M-185_(MISPC).svg *License*: Public Domain *Contributors*: User:IW4

File:Michigan H-33_Mackinac County.svg *Source*: http://bibliocm.bibliolabs.com/mwAnon/index.php?title=File:Michigan_H-33_Mackinac_County.svg *License*: Public Domain *Contributors*: User:IW4

File:Michigan H-40_Mackinac County.svg *Source*: http://bibliocm.bibliolabs.com/mwAnon/index.php?title=File:Michigan_H-40_Mackinac_County.svg *License*: Public Domain *Contributors*: User:IW4

File:Michigan H-42_Mackinac County.svg *Source*: http://bibliocm.bibliolabs.com/mwAnon/index.php?title=File:Michigan_H-42_Mackinac_County.svg *License*: Public Domain *Contributors*: User:IW4

File:Michigan H-57_Mackinac County.svg *Source*: http://bibliocm.bibliolabs.com/mwAnon/index.php?title=File:Michigan_H-57_Mackinac_County.svg *License*: Public Domain *Contributors*: User:IW4

File:Michigan H-63_Mackinac County.svg *Source*: http://bibliocm.bibliolabs.com/mwAnon/index.php?title=File:Michigan_H-63_Mackinac_County.svg *License*: Public Domain *Contributors*: User:IW4

File:Map of Michigan highlighting Schoolcraft County.svg *Source*: http://bibliocm.bibliolabs.com/mwAnon/index.php?title=File:Map_of_Michigan_highlighting_Schoolcraft_County.svg *License*: Public Domain *Contributors*: User:Dbenbenn

Image:US 2.svg *Source*: http://bibliocm.bibliolabs.com/mwAnon/index.php?title=File:US_2.svg *License*: Public Domain *Contributors*: SPUI, 1 anonymous edits

Image:M-77.svg *Source*: http://bibliocm.bibliolabs.com/mwAnon/index.php?title=File:M-77.svg *License*: Public Domain *Contributors*: User:IW4

Image:M-94.svg *Source*: http://bibliocm.bibliolabs.com/mwAnon/index.php?title=File:M-94.svg *License*: Public Domain *Contributors*: User:IW4

Image:M-149.svg *Source*: http://bibliocm.bibliolabs.com/mwAnon/index.php?title=File:M-149.svg *License*: Public Domain *Contributors*: User:IW4

Image:Michigan H-13 Alger County.svg *Source*: http://bibliocm.bibliolabs.com/mwAnon/index.php?title=File:Michigan_H-13_Alger_County.svg *License*: Public Domain *Contributors*: User:IW4

Image:Michigan H-42 Schoolcraft County.svg *Source*: http://bibliocm.bibliolabs.com/mwAnon/index.php?title=File:Michigan_H-42_Schoolcraft_County.svg *License*: Public Domain *Contributors*: User:IW4

Image:Michigan H-52 Schoolcraft County.svg *Source*: http://bibliocm.bibliolabs.com/mwAnon/index.php?title=File:Michigan_H-52_Schoolcraft_County.svg *License*: Public Domain *Contributors*: User:IW4

Image:DSCN4821 schoolcraftcountyroad e.jpg *Source*: http://bibliocm.bibliolabs.com/mwAnon/index.php?title=File:DSCN4821_schoolcraftcountyroad_e.jpg *License*: GNU Free Documentation License *Contributors*: Original uploader was Decumanus at en.wikipedia

File:Tahquamenon falls lower.jpg *Source*: http://bibliocm.bibliolabs.com/mwAnon/index.php?title=File:Tahquamenon_falls_lower.jpg *License*: Creative Commons Attribution 2.5 *Contributors*: User:anagy

File:Upper Tahquamenon Falls.jpg *Source*: http://bibliocm.bibliolabs.com/mwAnon/index.php?title=File:Upper_Tahquamenon_Falls.jpg *License*: Creative Commons Attribution 2.0 *Contributors*: James Phelps from USA

File:Tahquamenon_Falls1.JPG *Source*: http://bibliocm.bibliolabs.com/mwAnon/index.php?title=File:Tahquamenon_Falls1.JPG *License*: GNU Free Documentation License *Contributors*: User:Sujit kumar

File:2009-0618-TahquamenonFalls.jpg *Source*: http://bibliocm.bibliolabs.com/mwAnon/index.php?title=File:2009-0618-TahquamenonFalls.jpg *License*: Creative Commons Attribution 2.5 *Contributors*: Bobak Ha'Eri

File:Upper Tahquamenon falls Panoramic view.jpg *Source*: http://bibliocm.bibliolabs.com/mwAnon/index.php?title=File:Upper_Tahquamenon_falls_Panoramic_view.jpg *License*: Creative Commons Attribution-Sharealike 3.0 *Contributors*: User:Neocyberphile

file: MIMap-doton-Paradise.PNG *Source*: http://bibliocm.bibliolabs.com/mwAnon/index.php?title=File:MIMap-doton-Paradise.PNG *License*: GNU Free Documentation License *Contributors*: Original uploader was Seth Ilys at en.wikipedia

File:Upper Tahquamenon Falls (1).jpg *Source*: http://bibliocm.bibliolabs.com/mwAnon/index.php?title=File:Upper_Tahquamenon_Falls_(1).jpg *License*: Creative Commons Attribution-Sharealike 2.0 *Contributors*: Dawn Endico from Menlo Park, California

File:Tahquamenon Falls State Park, 1991.jpg *Source*: http://bibliocm.bibliolabs.com/mwAnon/index.php?title=File:Tahquamenon_Falls_State_Park,_1991.jpg *License*: Creative Commons Attribution-Sharealike 2.0 *Contributors*: Dawn Endico from Menlo Park, California

Image:YAM Sault Airport.jpg *Source*: http://bibliocm.bibliolabs.com/mwAnon/index.php?title=File:YAM_Sault_Airport.jpg *License*: GNU Free Documentation License *Contributors*: User:P199

CPSIA information can be obtained
at www.ICGtesting.com
Printed in the USA
LVHW060929250122
709154LV00024B/977